Evergrowing Evergreen

Evergrowing Evergreen

JILL BRISCOE

VICTOR BOOKS™

A DIVISION OF SCRIPTURE PRESS PUBLICATIONS INC.
USA CANADA ENGLAND

Scripture verses quoted are taken from *The New King James Version* (NKJV),
© 1979, 1980, 1982, Thomas Nelson, Inc., Publishers; the *Holy Bible, New International Version* (NIV), © 1973, 1978, 1984, International Bible Society, used by permission of Zondervan Bible Publishers; and the *King James Version* (KJV).

Recommended Dewey Decimal Classification: 223.2
Suggested Subject Heading: BIBLE, O.T.—PSALMS

Library of Congress Catalog Card Number: 86-60856
ISBN: 0-89693-255-9

VICTOR BOOKS
A division of SP Publications, Inc.
        Wheaton, Illinois 60187

·CONTENTS·

Recognition to Karen Seemuth
for assistance
in researching and formulating
parts of this book.

•BEFORE YOU BEGIN•

Women who gather together for Bible study are likely to be at different places in their spiritual lives, and their study materials should be flexible enough to meet their different needs. This book is designed to be used as a Bible study guide for such women's groups in homes or churches. It can also be used by women studying on their own. The lessons are written in five distinct sections, so that they can be used in a variety of situations. Groups and individuals alike can choose to use the elements they find most useful in the order they find most beneficial.

These studies will help you learn some new truths from the Bible as well as how to dig out those truths. You will learn not only *what* the Bible says, but how to use Scripture to deepen your relationship with Jesus Christ by obeying it and applying it in daily living. These studies will also provide an opportunity for potential leaders to learn how to lead a discussion in a nonthreatening setting.

What You'll Need

For each study you will need a Bible and this Bible study guide. You might also want to have a notebook in which to record your thoughts and discoveries from your personal study and group meetings. A notebook could also be used to record prayer requests from the group.

The Sections

Food for Thought. This is a devotional narrative that introduces the topic, person, or passage featured in the lesson. There are several ways it can be used. Each woman could read it before coming to the group meeting, and someone could briefly summarize it at the beginning. It could be read silently by each woman at the beginning of the session, or it could be read aloud, by one or several group members. (Suggested time: 10 minutes)

Talking It Over. This section contains discussion questions to help you review what you learned in Food for Thought. There are also questions to help you apply the narrative's truths to daily life. The person who leads the discussion of these questions need not be an experienced teacher. All that is needed is someone to keep things moving and facilitate group interaction. (Suggested time: 30 minutes)

7

Praying It Through. This is a list of suggestions for prayer based on the lesson. You may want to use all the suggestions or eliminate some in order to leave more time for personal sharing and prayer requests. (Suggested time: 20 minutes)

Digging Deeper. The questions in this section are also related to the passage, topic, or character from the lesson. But they will not always be limited to the exact passage or character from Food for Thought. Passages and characters from both the Old and New Testaments will appear in this section, in order to show how God has worked through *all* of history in people's lives. These questions will require a little more thinking and some digging into Scripture, as well as some use of Bible study tools. Participants will be stretched as they become experienced in the "how-tos" of Bible study. (Suggested time: 45 minutes)

Tool Chest. The Tool Chest contains a description of a specific type of Bible study help and includes an explanation of how it is used. An example of the tool is given, and an example of it or excerpt from it is usually included in the Digging Deeper study.

The Bible study helps in the Tool Chest can be purchased by anyone who desires to build a basic library of Bible study reference books and other tools. They would also be good additions to a church library. Some are reasonably inexpensive, but others are quite expensive. A few may be available in your local library or in a seminary or college library. A group might decide to purchase one tool during each series and build a corporate tool chest for all the members of the group to use. You can never be too young a Christian to begin to master Bible study helps, nor can you be too old to learn new methods of rightly dividing the Word of truth.

The Tool Chest won't be used during the group time unless the leader wishes to draw special attention to it. Those who will be using the Digging Deeper study should read the Tool Chest on their own before or after doing the study.

Options for Group Use

Different groups, made up of women at diverse stages of spiritual growth, will want to use the elements in this book in different ways. Here are a few suggestions to get you started, but be creative and sensitive to your group's needs.

□ Spend 5-15 minutes at the beginning of the group time introducing yourselves and having group members answer an icebreaker question. (Sample icebreaker questions are included under Tips for Leaders.)

□ Extend the prayer time to include sharing of prayer requests, praise items, or things the women have learned recently in their times of personal Bible study.

□ The leader could choose questions for discussion from the Digging Deeper section based on whether participants have prepared ahead of time or not.

□ The entire group could break into smaller groups to allow different groups to use different sections. (The smaller groups could move to other rooms in the home or church where you are meeting.)

The key thing to remember is that you *don't have to feel obliged to use everything*. Pick what you or your group needs. Omit questions or reword them if you wish. Feel free to be flexible!

Tips for Leaders

Preparation

1. Pray for the Holy Spirit's guidance as you study, that you will be equipped to teach the lesson and make it appealing and applicable.

2. Read through the entire lesson and any Bible passages or verses that are mentioned. Answer all the questions.

3. Become familiar enough with the lesson that, if time in the group is running out, you know which questions could most easily be left out.

4. Gather all the items you will need for the study: name tags, extra pens, extra Bibles.

The Meeting

1. Start and end on time.

2. Have everyone wear a name tag until group members know one another's names.

3. Have each woman introduce herself or ask regular attenders to introduce guests.

4. For each meeting, pick an icebreaker question or another activity to help the women get to know one another better.

5. Use any good ideas to make the women feel comfortable.

The Discussion

1. Ask the questions, but try to let the group answer. Don't be afraid of silence. Reword the question if it is unclear to the group or answer it yourself to clarify.

2. Encourage everyone to participate. If someone is shy ask her to answer an opinion question or another nonthreatening question. If

someone tends to monopolize the discussion, thank her for her contribution and ask if someone else has anything she would like to add. (Or ask her to make the coffee!)

3. If someone gives an incorrect answer, don't bluntly or tactlessly tell her so. If it is partly right, reinforce that. Ask if anyone else has any thoughts on the subject. (Disagree agreeably!)

4. Avoid tangents. If someone is getting off the subject, ask her how her point relates to the lesson.

5. Don't feel threatened if someone asks a question you can't answer. Tell her you don't know but will find out before the next meeting—then be sure to find out! Or ask if someone would like to research and present the answer at the group's next meeting.

Icebreaker Questions

The purpose of these icebreaker questions is to help the women in your group get to know one another over the course of the study. The questions you use when your group members don't know one another very well should be very general and nonthreatening. As time goes on, your questions can become more focused and specific. Always give the women the option of passing if they think a question is too personal.

What do you like to do for fun?

What is your favorite season? dessert? book?

What would be your ideal vacation?

What exciting thing happened to you this week?

What was the most memorable thing you did with your family when you were a child?

What one word best describes the way you feel today?

Tell three things you are thankful for.

Imagine that your house is on fire. What three things would you try to take with you on your way out?

If you were granted one wish, what would it be?

What experience of your past would you most enjoy reliving?

What quality do you most appreciate in a friend?

What is your pet peeve?

What is something you are learning to do or trying to get better at?

What is your greatest hope?

What is your greatest fear?

What one thing would you like to change about yourself?

What has been the greatest accomplishment of your life?

What has been the greatest disappointment of your life?

Need More Help?

Here is a list of books that contain helpful information on leading discussions and working in groups:

> *How to Lead Small Group Bible Studies* (NavPress, 1982).
> *Creative Bible Learning for Adults*, Monroe Marlowe and Bobbie Reed (Regal, 1977).
> *Getting Together*, Em Griffin (InterVarsity Press, 1982).
> *Good Things Come in Small Groups* (InterVarsity Press, 1985).

One Last Thought

This book is a tool you can use whether you have one or one hundred women who want to study the Bible and whether you have one or no teachers. Don't wait for a brilliant Bible study leader to appear—most such women acquired their skills by starting with a book like this and learning as they went along. Torrey said, "The best way to begin, is to begin." Happy beginnings!

PSALM 1

¹Blessed is the man
Who walks not in the counsel
   of the ungodly,
Nor stands in the path of sinners,
Nor sits in the seat of the scornful;

²But his delight is in the law of the
      LORD,
  And in His law he meditates day
    and night.

³He shall be like a tree
  Planted by the rivers of water,
   That brings forth its fruit in its
    season,
  Whose leaf also shall not wither;
And whatever he does shall prosper.

⁴The ungodly are not so,
But are like the chaff which the wind
    drives away.

⁵Therefore the ungodly shall not stand
    in the judgment,
Nor sinners in the congregation of the
    righteous.

⁶For the LORD knows the way of the
    righteous,
But the way of the ungodly shall
    perish.

1

The Lord My River

•FOOD FOR THOUGHT•

There are two sorts of men in this world—nowhere men and somewhere men. The nowhere man goes nowhere in life, yet in death heads somewhere that is actually nowhere forever. Back in the 60s the Beatles sang about the nowhere man in his nowhere land, making nowhere plans for nobody.

The psalmist sang about the nowhere man thousands of years before the Beatles ever got around to it! He described him as one who gets his advice from the ungodly (Ps. 1:1). We all know what sort of counsel that would be—ungodlike counsel.

The nowhere man turns to the opinion makers of his day to set his goals, and models his life after them. He watches the soaps, scans the magazines, and is a slave to Madison Avenue. I once talked with a woman who watched the soaps faithfully, hoping to find an answer to her own human dilemma. Her marriage was in jeopardy and the actors and actresses on the TV screen were in an almost identical situation to her own. "Perhaps I'll find an answer to my problem," she would say to herself, hoping against hope for some ray of light in her dark world.

Nowhere people hang around with sinners (Ps. 1:1, TLB). Sinners miss the mark, which is God's target of wholeness. The mark He wants us to hit is the mark of completeness—of Jesus-like living. People transgress—step beyond the boundaries the Lord has set for their behavior. Nowhere men are senseless and ruthless (Rom. 1:28, NIV). They all follow the same moral path. "Everybody's doing it," says the nowhere man, going along with the crowd. The nowhere man scoffs at the things of God, deriding those who have a religion. He makes a mockery of everything sacred and is, in fact, a believer in all unbelief. He puts Jesus and Jesus' friends down and snickers at preachers, church, and the Bible.

The nowhere man is described as chaff that the wind blows away (Ps. 1:4). The picture is vivid. Israel winnowed grain on a high hill to make full use of the wind. The farmer would use his winnowing fan to throw the grain high in the air and the chaff, which had no substance, would be carried away by the wind while the grain would fall safely down to be gathered and stored. One day Jesus our Judge will come. He will carry in His hand His winnowing fan, and all the people who have ever lived will be thrown up to the winds of God's judgment. Matthew 3:12 tells us that He will "thoroughly purge His floor." In Scripture, chaff stands as a picture of all that is weak and worthless. Nowhere men will be, on that day, on their way to nowhere forever; "they are not safe on Judgment Day" (Ps. 1:5, TLB).

Actions have consequences. What I do matters; therefore, what I am matters. "I am worth evaluating and judging," says the nowhere man proudly. "Quite so," God responds, "and I have already done it!" The Bible leaves no room for doubt about the matter—"the way of the ungodly shall perish" (Ps. 1:6). The nowhere man is warned by God's Word. If he does not recognize his predicament, come to his senses, and let Christ save him, his future will be like

> Solitary confinement
> With demons in alignment
> Endless deep
> Depressing
> Night
> A wild, weeping world without God!

But what of the somewhere man? Blessed is that man—the one among a thousand who lives to accomplish the end for which God created him. The somewhere man knows where he's going and how he's going to get there. That is because he possesses a map; he delights "in the law of the Lord" (Ps. 1:2). He studies this map and meditates on it long enough to know the way he should go. This is no mindless meditation either. He spends day and night charting the course of his life.

He listens not to the cynical or ungodly man, but rather to the Lord. The somewhere man is not likened to chaff. Rather, he is like a tree planted by rivers of water. Isaiah called this kind of person "a planting of the Lord" (Isa. 61:3). He is bound to be productive, regularly producing luscious fruit.

Many young Christians after finding Jesus as their Saviour instantly produce one bumper crop of fruit. Then for months there may be nothing but leaves. Those who learn to meditate on the map prosper spiritually, bearing consistently the fruit of God's Spirit—Christian character.

Somewhere men and women are not only planted and productive, they are pretty too! Psalm 1:3 tells us they will be like a tree whose "leaf also shall not wither." They will, in fact, be evergreen! "The trees of the Lord are full of sap" (Ps. 104:16). That is, of course, if their roots are continually in the river.

During a particularly frantic week I was thinking about this and penned a simple poem to remind myself of how important it is to keep my life rooted in the river of God.

EVERGREEN
(Psalm 1)

O Lord, I'd bear some fruit for Thee
If I could just stand still
And let my roots grow deep and wide
Entwined around Thy will.
I'd need to learn to wait for Thee,
To whisper to my heart;
I'd have to let the Holy Ghost
Have all, not just a part.

The problem, Lord, I have is this,
I cannot stand quite still;
Too many other neat tree friends
Are planted on my hill.
I feel a little guilty
But I've only me to thank;
I'm far too busy rushing
Up and down my river bank.

There's Myrtle, Rose, and Holly
Who are friends of mine you know;
We're so busy having fellowship,
We have no time to grow.
There are the cutest little saplings,
The sweetest things to nurse,
There's little time to meditate
On chapter and verse.

Now I've grown to be an expert
On blight and stunted trees,
So I run expensive seminars
With spiritual expertise.
I tell willows not to wallow
And chestnuts not to crack,
So I'm far too tired to watch and pray
By the time that I get back.

O Lord, don't chop me down
And use my trunk for firewood;
I'd love to stop my frantic pace
And settle, if I could.
Take hold my tree and planteth me;
Don't let my green leaves wither.
Oh, let my thirsty branches drink
Cool water from Thy river.

Dear King of forest glades and glen,
O tree King, I adore Thee;
I'll take root where I am planted,
Content to bring Thee glory.
O Spirit, cause my leaves to shine,
True fruit at last be seen,
I yield to Thee—Oh, touch my tree
And keep me evergreen.

King Solomon planted magnificent gardens in his time. He made rivers and reservoirs and lined them with citrus trees, which displayed luscious evergreen leaves. When I ask Christ to be my Saviour, He plants in me the Holy Spirit who is like God's refreshing river. The Lord becomes my river of life. Revelation 22:1-2 speaks of "a river of the water of life," coming out from the throne of God. The leaves of the trees planted on either side of the river display greenery that is for the healing of the nations. Ezekiel, in his vision, also sees a river. This river is flowing out from the temple, and we're told that "where the river flows everything will live" (Ezek. 47:1, 9).

I have to ask myself, "Do my leaves heal people's hurts? Does everything around me spring to life, and if not, where are my roots?"

God is the river of life and also of laughter. Have you ever noticed that where the river flows everyone will laugh? Psalm 46:4 says, "There is a river whose streams make glad the city of God, the holy place where the Most High dwells." And Psalm 36:8 says, "They feast on the abundance of your house; you give them drink from your river of delights."

Do our twigs twitter and our leaves rustle with rejoicing? I do not speak of jollity—a shallow effervescence of silliness—but rather of inlaid joy, a deep implanting of my Saviour's pleasure in my soul.

What's more, wherever the river flows, there is liberty. Jeremiah 17:7-8 speaks of the tree planted by the water in this way:

> Blessed is the man that trusteth in the Lord, and whose hope the Lord is. For he shall be as a tree planted by the waters, and that spreadeth out her roots by the river, and shall not see when heat cometh, but her leaf shall be green; and shall not be careful in the year of drought, neither shall cease from yielding fruit.

Some time ago I retreated with some fellow believers for a weekend of renewal. I thought I knew them all well, but as we shared together, I discovered that for many of them, the past year had been a year of drought. One had been through the pain of divorce. Another had lost a father to cancer. A close friend didn't yet know the whereabouts of her runaway child. And one woman had endured the outrage of "battering." Yet these women had faithfully served the Lord by my side in our church. I can vouch for the fact that they had not been "worry trees," wringing their twigs to bits, but rather, they never failed to be evergreen! More than that, their leaves had indeed been used for the healing of other people's ills. They were so unlike the little desert scrub brush that Jeremiah paints for us with such stark contrast:

> Cursed is the one who trusts in man, who depends on flesh for his strength and whose heart turns away from the Lord. He will be like a bush in the wastelands; he will not see prosperity when it comes. He will dwell in the parched places of the desert, in a salt land where no one lives (Jer. 17:5-6, NIV).

Tell me, are you a nowhere man or a somewhere man? Let me pose the question another way:

Little scrub brush
Never thriving,

Winds and sand forever driving
    in your face.

Little scrub brush
Never growing,
Never flowering, never knowing
    sheltered place.

Salty soil a thirst creating,
Never quenching or abating—
    Little scrub brush

Wouldn't you like to be
Like yonder stately tree?

It's really quite simple. A somewhere man is a nowhere man who comes to Someone who can make a difference in his life—Christ. Christ is the Saviour who forgives our "nowhereness" and gives us eternal life. If you haven't done so already, why don't you ask Him to plant you by the river? Then let your roots go down deep in Him.

•TALKING IT OVER•

1. READ AND DISCUSS.　　　　　　　　　　*12 minutes*
   As a group, read Psalm 1. Then discuss these
   questions:
   ☐ How is the wicked man like chaff?
   ☐ How is the righteous man like a tree?
   ☐ How is the Bible like a map?

2. MEDITATE.　　　　　　　　　　　　　　*6 minutes*
   To *meditate* means "to chew over till digested."
   ☐ On your own, read Psalm 1 again. Really con-
      centrate on its meaning.
   ☐ Choose one verse from Psalm 1 that you espe-
      cially like. Close your eyes and think about it.
      Why do you like that verse so much?
   ☐ Look at the psalm one more time, asking God
      to show you something in your life that is
      wrong. Close your eyes and think about it.
      What can you do to right that wrong?
   ☐ If you finish this exercise before the others in
      the group, read Joshua 1:8. Meditate on it.
      Memorize it.

3. SHARE.　　　　　　　　　　　　　　　*6 minutes*
   In twos or as a whole group, share the things you
   have been thinking about.

4. PRAY INDIVIDUALLY.　　　　　　　　　*6 minutes*
   The Lord is your river. You are His tree. Talk
   to Him using these and other symbols found in
   Psalm 1. For example, you might pray something
   like, "Lord, You are my river—the source of my
   refreshment. I feel so withered, insecure, as if my
   roots are lying on the surface of my Christianity,"
   and so on.

•PRAYING IT THROUGH•

Divide into small groups. (Six is a good number for a small group.) Let each group appoint a leader.

Suggested Times

1. (Leader) Let each member of your group read a different passage from those listed below (all of them have to do with trees or rivers).
   - ☐ Psalm 36:8
   - ☐ Psalm 46:4
   - ☐ Proverbs 3:18

   Take 5 minutes to "chew over" the meanings of the symbols in these verses. Then spend 5 minutes in praise. Help yourself with the words you have been reading. Make them yours.

   10 minutes

2. (Leader) Read verse 5 of Psalm 1, which speaks of judgment. As a group, pray for nowhere people you know and love. Keep your prayers brief. (Leader) Feel free to say Amen if someone's prayer lasts longer than a minute.

   5 minutes

3. (Leader) Ask a group member to read Psalm 1:3, having to do with staying evergreen. You may want to choose someone who hasn't prayed (it's easier to read than pray!). As a group, spend some time praying for "withering" Christians you know. Also petition God for evergreen church leaders.

   5 minutes

4. Take time to pray for specific matters you as individuals are concerned about. Then close by praying together the Lord's Prayer.

   10 minutes

   Our Father who art in heaven, hallowed be Thy name.
   Thy kingdom come. Thy will be done in earth,
   As it is in heaven.
   Give us this day our daily bread.
   And forgive us our debts, as we forgive our debtors.
   And lead us not into temptation,
   But deliver us from evil:
   For Thine is the kingdom, and the power,
   And the glory, forever. Amen.

•DIGGING DEEPER•

Introduction to the Book of Psalms

The psalms were written over a long period of time. David wrote many of them; others are attributed to Solomon, Asaph, the sons of Korah, and Moses. The Book of Psalms is a book of poetry. Set to music, the Hebrew people used the psalms as hymns for both public and private worship. The psalms record a history of the nation of Israel. Christ classed the psalms with the Law and the Prophets.

The psalms can be grouped in five different categories:

Community hymns.
This type of psalm includes a call to praise, praise for the Lord's deeds and attributes, and a conclusion. Some examples of community hymns are Psalms 19, 84, and 117.

Thanksgiving songs of the individual.
These psalms include introductory statements of thanksgiving or praise, descriptions of distress, confessions of the Lord as redeemer/deliverer, vows of praise, and a conclusion. Psalms 18, 34, and 116 are a few examples of thanksgiving songs of the individual.

Lament of the individual.
Each of these psalms includes an invocation or address to God, a complaint or lament, a confession of trust, a petition, and a vow of praise. Thirty percent of the psalms fit into this category. Three examples of this type of psalm are Psalms 10, 51, and 88.

Lament of the community.
This type of psalm includes a lament or complaint, a prayer to God to remove the calamity, and a statement of certainty of the Lord's hearing. Some examples of psalms of lament of the community are Psalms 44, 74, and 80.

Royal psalms.
These psalms show the relationship between God and the king. Some of the royal psalms are messianic psalms. A few examples of royal psalms are Psalms 2, 20, and 72.

1. Read the following psalms and decide which category each of them belongs to:

   Psalm 32

   Psalm 45

   Psalm 48

   Psalm 79

   Psalm 102

   Psalm 1 is a prologue or introduction to the entire Book of Psalms. It emphasizes the importance of having a proper attitude toward the Law of the Lord.

2. Psalm 1:1 describes the man of God and what he does *not* do. He does not deviate from the ways of God, conforming to the world. He does not accept the world's advice, nor is party to the world's ways, adopting the world's attitudes.

   Here is an example of what a man or woman of God would *not* say: "It's OK for me to steal from the company I work for. They'll never miss it. Besides, I'm underpaid."

   Now give two more examples of what people of God would not do or say.

   Example:

   Example:

3. What characterizes the scoffer?

Proverbs 1:22

Proverbs 9:7

Proverbs 9:8, 12

Proverbs 13:1

Proverbs 14:6

Proverbs 21:24

Proverbs 29:8

How should a scoffer be treated?

Psalm 1:1

Proverbs 19:25

Proverbs 21:11

Proverbs 22:10

What is the scoffer's basic sin?

Proverbs 21:24

What is the scoffer's punishment?

Proverbs 3:34

Proverbs 19:29

4. If you were to look up the word *water* in *The New Bible Dictionary* (Eerdmans, First Edition, p. 1317), you would read:

In a part of the world where water is in short supply, it naturally features significantly in the lives of the people of the Bible. Nothing is more serious to them than absence of water, and conversely rainfall is a sign of God's favour and goodness. An equally serious menace to life is water that has been polluted or rendered undrinkable. . . . Frequently water is symbolical of God's blessing and of spiritual refreshment, and the longing for it indicates spiritual need.

Why is the image of a tree planted by streams of water so vivid in the Israelite setting?

Read John 4:1-14 and John 7:37-39. What does water represent in these passages?

5. Looking up the words *agriculture* and *chaff* in the same Bible dictionary you'd read:

To harvest the crop, the grain was grasped in one hand and then cut with the sickle held in the other hand. These bundles were tied into sheaves, which in turn were loaded on to donkeys or camels to be carried to the threshing-floor. . . . Gleaners followed the reapers, and then animals were let into the stubble in the following order: sheep, goats, and camels.
Threshing-floors were located near the village at a point where the winds would be helpful for winnowing.

The floor itself was either a rock outcropping or a soil area coated with marly clay. The sheaves were scattered about a foot deep over the floor and protected at the edges by a ring of stones. The animals, which were sometimes shod for this purpose, were driven round and round until the grain was loosened and the stocks chipped into small pieces. A faster method was to use a wooden sled with stones or iron fragments fastened into the under side. The grain was winnowed by tossing it into the wind with wooden pitchforks. The grain might be sifted then before being bagged for human use. The straw was saved as fodder for the animals (*The New Bible Dictionary,* pp. 19-20).

* * * * * * * * * *

Chaff denotes worthless husks and broken straw blown away by the wind during the winnowing of grain (*The New Bible Dictionary,* p. 203).

How do chaff and the firmly planted tree differ?

How does the "blessed" person differ from the "wicked" person?

6. What is meant by "the wicked will not stand in the judgment"? (Ps. 1:5)

7. If doing this study as a group, break into smaller groups of two or three people each and discuss these questions:
   □ Why is it hard to believe in a God who judges?
   □ What are some positive aspects of judgment?

25

8. Read the following verses:

   Galatians 3:26-27
   Galatians 4:5-6
   Galatians 5:5
   Philippians 3:9

   According to the passages you've just read, how does a person become righteous?

9. What do *you* delight in?

10. What kind of fruit is *your life* bringing forth?

•TOOL CHEST•
(A Suggested Optional Resource)

BIBLE DICTIONARY

One of the most valuable tools available at the present time is the Bible dictionary. It is used in much the same way as an English language dictionary but contains much more information for most entries. To use such a tool you need only to look up the word or subject in question, and the dictionary will guide you from there. For instance, if you were reading about the church at Philadelphia in Revelation 3:7-13, you would need to understand something more about the city of Philadelphia to understand the passage. The description of the city vividly illuminates what Christ was saying to that church because the Lord used imagery that was familiar to those Philadelphian believers.

The New Bible Dictionary (Eerdmans) was featured in the Digging Deeper section of this chapter. Besides that Bible dictionary, here are the titles of a couple of other ones you might use from time to time. Both of these dictionaries are available through Christian bookstores: *Unger's Bible Dictionary* by Merrill F. Unger (Moody Press, 1957). This one-volume, 1200-page dictionary includes 536 photographs and drawings and 16 multicolored maps. In 1963, Zondervan published its *Pictorial Bible Dictionary* (Merrill C. Tenney, general editor). This is also a valuable resource for students of Scripture.

Next time you come across a word or subject in Scripture you don't understand or would like to know more about, consult your Bible dictionary.

PSALM 18

¹I will love You, O LORD, my strength.

²The LORD, is my rock and my fortress
   and my deliverer;
My God, my strength, in whom I will trust;
My shield and the horn of my salvation,
   my stronghold.

³I will call upon the LORD,
   who is worthy to be praised;
So shall I be saved from my enemies.

⁴The pangs of death encompassed me,
And the floods of ungodliness made me afraid.

⁵The sorrows of Sheol surrounded me;
The snares of death confronted me.

⁶In my distress I called upon the LORD,
And cried out to my God;
He heard my voice from His temple, even to His ears.
. . . .

³⁰As for God, His way is perfect;
   The Word of the LORD is proven;
   He is a shield to all who trust in Him.

³¹For who is God, except the LORD?
   And who is a rock, except our God?

³²It is God who arms me with strength,
   And makes my way perfect.

³³He makes my feet like the feet of deer,
   And sets me on my high places.

³⁴He teaches my hands to make war,
   So that my arms can bend a bow of bronze.

³⁵You have also given me the shield of Your salvation;
   Your right hand has held me up,
   Your gentleness has made me great.

³⁶You enlarged my path under me;
   So that my feet did not slip.
. . . .

⁴⁶The LORD lives! Blessed be my Rock!
   Let the God of my salvation be exalted.

2

The Lord My Rock

•FOOD FOR THOUGHT•

David wrote Psalm 18 after the Lord delivered him from all his enemies. In this psalm he talked of being in the heights of ecstasy as well as in the depths of despair. So often David found therapy for his hurting heart by taking up his pen and pouring out his complaints to God. As he wrote, the dark places were remembered rather than experienced, and he was glad.

So often, like the nine lepers who forgot to return to the Lord Jesus to say thank you (Luke 17:11-19), we go on our way healed and helped, forgetting the One responsible for the happy outcome of our difficulties. Not so with David. Invariably, like the one grateful leper, he returned to bow before the Lord his Maker and give Him praise.

Any passage of Scripture that deals with the heights and depths of spiritual experience is well worth looking at. Both extremes are part and parcel of our everyday lives; both need addressing. How do we behave when "all is well" with our souls? Paradoxically, we often flounder in the good times, possibly because we do not have to depend, to cling, to claim help from the Lord who is our Rock. On the other hand, we don't do very well in the bad times either, mainly because we haven't learned to do well in the good times! To know the reality of God in the day of trouble and sorrow is not a skill that is learned instantly the day my father dies, a child runs away from home, or I lose my job. David wisely learned his lessons in the "light" and therefore saw his way home when "darkness" fell. Don't you want to know how to do that—how to stay close to God on the hills so you can sense His presence in the hollows? I know I do! In Psalm 18 we find the clues to David's success.

Psalm 18 is also recorded in 2 Samuel 22 with slight variations. Though it cannot be proved, it is suggested that some of the wording in 2 Samuel 22 was changed in this psalm for use in public worship. Notice that in the superscription the psalm mentions being delivered from "all" his enemies. Written during a period of time when his life was crowned with almost unbroken success, David is careful to begin by saying that the blessings of the Lord have resulted in a love for God that sweeps his senses and leaves him exulting in God's character and intervention on his behalf. Using *rāhám*, a word that means "to love very tenderly as with a mother's love," David mentions that the rocklike characteristics of his God are the very aspects of His person that have called forth that response from him. "I will love You, Oh Lord, my strength," he sings, "[You are] my rock, my fortress and my deliverer" (Ps. 18:1-2, NIV).

The term *rock*, as it pertains to God, is one of David's most used metaphors. Perhaps he drew his word pictures and metaphors from the rugged rock-strewn countryside that was as much a part of him as his name. In Psalm 40, David uses the picture of a rock in a most graphic fashion:

> I waited patiently for the Lord; and He inclinded unto me, and heard my cry. He brought me up also out of a horrible pit, out of the miry clay, and set my feet upon a rock, and established my goings. And He hath put a new song in my mouth, even praise unto our God; many shall see it, and fear, and shall trust in the Lord" (Ps. 40:1-3, KJV).

Here he speaks of a new depth of despair he has experienced: it's a horrible pit, as miry clay, a sink hole that can't be escaped, no solid ground. Then he sings of new heights: "He brought me up . . . and set my feet upon a rock, and established my goings." Now *that's* something to sing about! The "new song" our Rock gives us to sing after such experiences is a sound of salvation that finds its way into many a heart. In verse 3, David assures us that "many shall see it, and fear, and shall trust in the Lord."

That brings to mind Isaiah 32. Here a situation is described concerning the reign of righteous kings. The prophet explains that as each man obeys a righteous king he will become a blessing to others around him. In fact, each will be protective of others, like a "shadow of a great rock within a weary land" (Isa. 32:2). David knew that a shadow is an inescapable companion, an exact representation of the object it shadows. If we can be shadows of the Mighty Rock to others, then many who are stumbling through the dry deserts of this world, desperate for some sight of strong stability on the horizon, will be helped by the sense of safety and strength we can bring them. We can then tell them about the Lord who is the Rock of our salvation.

What are some of the characteristics of a rock? The word *rock* certainly brings to mind a sense of *permanence*. Didn't Jesus Himself tell a story of a wise man who built his house on a rock? "Everyone who hears these words of Mine and puts them into practice is like a wise man," Jesus told His hearers (Matt. 7:24). Those who build on the Rock have a firm foundation for their lives. Jesus warned, however, that those who build their lives on the sand have a "shifting" style of living that will certainly collapse around their most cherished hopes and dreams when the storms come (Matt. 7:26-27).

Our Lord also said that those who stayed close to Him—as close as shadows—would reflect this rocklike quality. He told Peter that He would craft this quality out of his character so that others would be helped by it. Simon would fail many times before becoming Peter, the rock. But Christ promised him that after his failures, and when he was "converted," he "would strengthen [his] brethren" (Luke 22:32). In this day and age when permanence is in short demand, living a life of spiritual stability is a great way to attract people to the Gospel.

The word *rock* also reminds me of *perspective*. When visiting friends in Arizona or Colorado, I am always amazed at the way the houses are precariously placed on the peaks and summits of the mountains or on the sides of hills, giving a breathtaking panoramic view of God's incredible creation. Building our house on the Spiritual Rock who is Christ (1 Cor. 10:4), certainly gives us that good perspective on life that is necessary if we are going to have a clear vision and understanding of our environment.

Having our feet solidly planted on Him gives us a heavenly perspective on the things of earth. Not only can we see the beauty around us, we can see the beast as well. When the Prophet Elijah needed to regroup and recoup, he travelled many miles through the desert until he came to Mt. Horeb. It was on that mountain he found a new perspective, or to be more accurate, regained his old one! He understood again—perhaps more clearly—the purposes of God and his part in them, and he received the strength needed to continue to be God's man for the moment (1 Kings 19:3-9). We need to remember that when we, like Elijah, are "pooped prophets" who have lost sight of God and His purposes among men, that we can flee "to the Rock that is higher" than we are (Ps. 61:2). He will lift us up, and give us new eyes, new hearts, and new songs to sing.

The word *rock* also gives me a picture of *protection*.

Rock of Ages, cleft for me,
Let me hide myself in Thee.

God is our Rock. He is the *right* Rock as Moses points out in Deuteronomy 32:4. He is also the *rejected* Rock (32:15, 18). But because of His redemptive work on our behalf, He becomes to the believer a *renewing* Rock (32:47). The New Testament confirms this picture; Christ is our Rock: "the living Stone—rejected by men but chosen by God and precious to Him" (1 Peter 2:4). Peter goes on to say that to those who don't believe, Christ is "a stone that causes men to stumble and a rock that makes them fall."

Now is the day of salvation. There is still opportunity for all of us to run to Him for protection, to plead His shed blood for us, to beg His mercy for our many sins. He, as David rightly says, will be a refuge and a resource for all who call on Him (Ps. 18:2).

As David looks back over the manifold goodness of God, he cannot help but burst forth in an exultant song of praise. The sorrow is over and the celebration has begun. What God has been to David in the depths, He will be to David on the heights. Counting our many blessings is excellent medicine for the heart. Counting our many trials can be too, especially when they bring to mind the Lord who has been "my rock, my fortress, my deliverer; my God, my strength . . . my shield, and the horn of my salvation, and my stronghold" (Ps. 18:2). These sorts of remembrances have to result in a song of love!

•TALKING IT OVER•

1. READ AND DISCUSS TOGETHER.   *20 minutes*
   ☐ Read Psalm 40:1-3 as a group. Though David   (3 minutes)
   literally experienced the things these verses
   speak about, Psalm 40 is a messianic psalm,
   relating to the One who truly went down to the
   "pit" for us, and yet was "brought up" by God
   through the Resurrection.

   ☐ Now read Hebrews 4:14-16 and discuss these   (5 minutes)
   questions: What does Hebrews 4:14-16 have to
   do with Psalm 40:1-3? What do the truths of
   these passages combined have to do with us?

   ☐ Next read Deuteronomy 32:1-4 and discuss   (7 minutes)
   these questions: What do you learn about Moses' teaching? (vv. 1-3) What do you learn about
   the God of Moses? (v. 4) What principles
   should we apply to our own teaching?

   ☐ Finally, read Deuteronomy 32:4, 18, 30-31, 37. (5 minutes)
   Then come up with a list of additional thoughts
   from these verses about God our Rock.

2. FOLLOW THROUGH.   *5 minutes*
   (Complete this part of the exercise in twos.) Use
   the following New Testament verses to follow
   through on the theme of God as our Rock. What
   do these verses teach you that you didn't learn
   from the Old Testament verses you looked at
   earlier?
   1 Peter 2:6-8
   Ephesians 2:20
   1 Corinthians 1:23; Romans 9:32-33
   Matthew 21:42-44

3. PRAY.   *5 minutes*
   How has God been your Rock recently? Using
   Psalm 18:2 as your basis for prayer, thank God for
   being your Rock.

•PRAYING IT THROUGH•

---

1. Praise God for: *10 minutes*
   - ☐ The heights and the depths.
   - ☐ Lessons learned there.
   - ☐ Faith that was strengthened.
   - ☐ The stability of God's presence and power at all times.

---

2. Pray by name (first name only) for: *10 minutes*
   - ☐ People who are in sink holes of their own making, or who are in sink holes not of their own making.
   - ☐ Missionaries and church leaders—that their lives would be "shadows" of their Rock. Pray for yourself in this regard also.
   - ☐ People you know who are living on the heights, who have forgotten God in their prosperity.
   - ☐ Some whose love for God has grown cold— pray that their love will be renewed as they "remember His goodness."

---

3. Read Psalm 18 to yourself. Then make up your own psalm of praise as you review your past.   *10 minutes*

•DIGGING DEEPER•

Background to Psalm 18

Psalm 18 can be divided into sections that are *autobiographical* in nature—David relates some of the experiences of his life, giving personal testimony to the faithfulness and help of God, His Rock—and sections that concentrate more on the *eternal character and nature of God*.

1. Divide into twos. Look at *one* of the following sections from Psalm 18 with its corresponding background reference from the life of David. (We do not know if these background references are the exact experiences David had in mind when writing this psalm, but certainly they are examples of the kinds of situations in which David found himself.)

Psalm 18:4-6	1 Samuel 23:7-18
Psalm 18:16-19	1 Samuel 23:21-29
Psalm 18:32-36	1 Samuel 30:1-20
Psalm 18:37-42	2 Samuel 5:17-25
Psalm 18:43-45	2 Samuel 8:1-14

2. In pairs, spend a few moments meditating on the references you selected. Visualize the situation David is faced with in your background reference, and write down what you learn from David's attitude toward the situation, as expressed in your reference from Psalm 18.

3. What do these references teach you about God, our Rock?

4. Report briefly on whay you have found to the rest of the group.

The Character of Our Rock

"David my servant . . . will call out to me, 'You are my Father, my God, the Rock my Saviour' " (Ps. 89:20, 26). In Psalm 18, and in other psalms you will study in this part of the lesson, David *does* cry out to the Lord, his Rock.

5. Name as many characteristics of our rocklike God as you can from the following verses in Psalm 18. When necessary, supply your own word for the characteristic being described. For example, for verse 31 you might substitute the word *supreme* in place of the phrase, "For who is God besides the Lord?"

   (vv. 1-3)

   (vv. 7-15)

   (vv. 25-27)

   (vv. 30-31)

6. Many aspects of God's character are described here, but in one sense, the picture of God as our Rock is a fusion of them all. Choose *one* characteristic of God our Rock from your list in question 5, and share briefly with the rest of the group how God has proved to be your Rock in a particular situation.

7. In each of the psalms listed below, David cries out to the Lord, his Rock. As time allows, answer the following two questions for each of the psalms listed. ☐ Which category of psalm does this psalm belong to? (Refer back to "Introduction to the Book of Psalms" in the Digging Deeper section of chapter 1. Be careful to read the whole psalm before recording your choice of category.) ☐ What characteristics of the Rock does David describe here? (Examples are given.)

Psalm 28

Category _____

Characteristics <u>Example: a Rock who hears</u> (vv. 1, 6)

_____ (v.   )

_____ (v.   )

_____ (v.   )

Psalm 31

Category _____

Characteristics <u>Example: a redeeming Rock</u> (v. 5   )

_____ (v.   )

_____ (v.   )

_____ (v.   )

_____ (v.   )

_____ (v.   )

_____ (v.   )

_____ (v.   )

_____ (v.   )

Psalm 61

Category _____

Characteristics <u>Example: a higher Rock</u> (v. 2   )

_____ (v.   )

_____ (v.   )

_____ (v.   )

_____ (v.   )

8. Review your list. How does your knowledge of this God compare with David's?

9. Come up with three of your *own* descriptions for the God of your experience, and share them with the group. For example, you might say that your God is *a Rock of stability.*
   Your descriptions: _____

   _____

   _____

10. Which of David's descriptions of the Lord, our Rock, do you feel you most need to discover now for a particular situation you are facing? Share this with the group, perhaps giving a brief word of explanation. Then close by praying for one another.

•TOOL CHEST•
(A Suggested Optional Resource)

BIOGRAPHICAL BOOKS

A whole range of books is available today that are "biographical" in their approach to Bible study. These books tend to focus on one or more Bible characters with a view to bringing them to life for us and to drawing from their experiences eternal, spiritual truths.

Some of these books are written in easy-to-read narrative styles that draw you into the heart of the action and right into the skin of the characters, enabling you to empathize with and understand them in a new light. "Paper" figures become *real* people.

When used as background for the passages you are studying, these books can be invaluable resources, informing you of historical contexts and firing up your imagination so that people, places, and events take on flesh and animation.

The best of these books use God-given imagination to help you read between the lines of Scripture while always seeking to be faithful and accurate to the biblical record. They also highlight important spiritual lessons to be learned from particular Bible characters.

In choosing a suitable book of this kind, be careful that accuracy is a high priority for the author! If you are in doubt as to the author's theological point of view, stick with well-known Christian publishers who have well-established theological reputations.

For biographical material on the life of David, we have recommended some excellent books in the bibliographic section below. These books range in approach from Bible study to storytelling. Each in its own way will enrich your meditation on David's psalms by helping you see them against the backdrop of his experiences.

W. Phillip Keller in his book on the life of David says, "David was now suddenly to be thrust into a life of great adventure and dire peril. To the end of his long years he would know only war, bloodshed, and enormous anguish of spirit. Yet out of such unpromising material God would bring tremendous honor, fame, wealth, blessing, and beauty of language never matched in another human being."

Biographies about David

Stuart Briscoe, *A Heart for God* (Nashville: Thomas Nelson).
W. Phillip Keller, *David: The Time of Saul's Tyranny* (Waco, Tex.: Word, 1985).
F.B. Meyer, *David* (Ft. Washington, Pa.: Christian Literature Crusade, 1979).
Alan Redpath, *The Making of a Man of God* (Old Tappan, NJ: Revell, 1979).

PSALM 23

[1]The LORD is my shepherd;
I shall not want.

[2]He makes me to lie down in green
   pastures;
He leads me beside the still waters.

[3]He restores my soul;
He leads me in the paths of
   righteousness
For His name's sake.

[4]Yea, though I walk through the valley
   of the shadow of death,
I will fear no evil;
For You are with me;
Your rod and Your staff,
   they comfort me.

[5]You prepare a table before me in the
   presence of my enemies;
You anoint my head with oil;
My cup runs over.

[6]Surely goodness and mercy shall
   follow me
All the days of my life;
And I will dwell in the house
   of the LORD
Forever.

3
The Lord My Shepherd

•FOOD FOR THOUGHT•

Of all the symbols Jesus used to describe Himself—the Vine, the Door, the Way, the Truth, the Life, the Light of the world—none has greater impact than that of the Shepherd. Many, many people find this concept appealing, comforting, and challenging. Perhaps we like to think of our Lord as Shepherd because, admitting to our own sheeplike natures, we recognize our need for His tender care and guidance. Or maybe it's the thought of God's shepherding arms around us as He rescues us from some dark hole of our own making that bring a sense of security to our souls. The Lord certainly gave us much to think about concerning the relationship between the Shepherd and His sheep. "I am the gate for the sheep," He told His disciples (John 10:7). His followers knew very well that an Eastern shepherd would lie down across the entrance to the sheep pen becoming, himself, the gate—the human barrier that would protect the defenseless flock from predators. Jesus was using a word picture that was to become an appalling reality. Our Lord knew that the lion, a picture of Satan, would have to kill the Shepherd and scatter the flock if He (Jesus) was to become the very door of heaven for us. He also knew the old lion would find Jesus easy prey. Pinned to the Cross by hammer and nails, Jesus would choose not to defend Himself. "The Good Shepherd lays down His life for the sheep," Jesus told His friends (John 10:11).

We can imagine Jesus' thoughts reaching out to the psalms of David for encouragement as He hanged on the Cross. And what better psalm from which to gain strength than Psalm 22? It so graphically portrayed His crucifixion.

David could never have known his words would be borrowed by Christ in His extremity. A shepherd himself, David would be thinking only of his own troubles as he penned the twenty-second Psalm

41

and sent it to his musical director, telling him to set it to the tune of "The Doe of the Morning." David must have know from his own experience what it was like to be hunted like a hind and to be helpless in the face of his enemies who appeared to be like wild animals. On Calvary, Jesus too came to know in His own experience what that was like. "My God, my God, why have You forsaken me?" He cried (Ps. 22:1; Matt. 27:46). "Roaring lions tearing their prey open their mouths wide against me" (Ps. 22:13), and again in Psalm 22:21, "Rescue me from the mouth of the lions." Jesus, knowing that awful sense of isolation at the beginning of His agony, cried out to His Father for help. In truth, on Good Friday "the lion got Him!"

Our Lord used the sense of the words of Psalm 22 when He said, "It is finished!" and with that He dismissed His Spirit into His Father's hands (John 19:30). Listen to the triumphant, upbeat turn of David's psalm: "Posterity will serve Him; future generations will be told about the Lord. They will proclaim His righteousness to a people yet unborn—for *He has done it*" (Ps. 22:30-31). In other words, on Good Friday "the lion got Him," but on Easter Sunday morning "He got the lion!" God raised Jesus from the dead and placed Him at His own right hand on high (1 Peter 3:22). Today, the Good Shepherd, having given His life for the sheep, lives on to guide His followers through the valleys of life into the heavenly fold.

A brief glance at Psalm 23 shows us some of the expectations the heavenly Shepherd has for His sheep. First, we learn that He would have us lie down often in green pastures (a beautiful picture of the Word of God). It takes time to graze to our satisfaction. Too many of us tend to whip through the nourishment that He provides for us, snatching a blade of grass on the way to more selfish pursuits. But what we really need is to settle into a spiritually stable "feeding pattern," if we are going to develop our earthly relationship with our heavenly Shepherd.

Next, we must experience what it is to be led by "quiet waters" (Ps. 23:2). God works in quiet power. In Genesis 1:2, we read that "the Spirit of God moved upon the face of the waters." In this verse, we get a sense of His quiet, creative power at work. Think of it—the eye of the storm is an incredibly still place. We must "be still and know that [He] is God" (Ps. 46:10), taking precious moments out of our busy schedules to spend with Him. This will mean a lot of practical planning on our parts, requiring that we exercise our wills to carry out our inner promises to the Spirit of God. Habits become habits only with practice! Sometimes it helps to meet God with someone else for a time, until the habit is well established and we trust ourselves to meet God on our own. Sheep can help sheep sometimes.

Taking time to be with the Shepherd is essential because life is very confusing at times. Life is made up of many paths and cross-roads. People make bad choices, and yet, it doesn't have to be that way. It helps to ask yourself, "Will this thing I am about to do honor the Shepherd?" If it will, then you can do it, but if, in fact, it will do harm to the Shepherd's name, then you must not do it. Sheep that belong to the Good Shepherd want others to see that He never leads them to do the wrong thing. When we make our choices, it is the Shepherd's reputation that is at stake. For example, the Shepherd would never lead us to walk into an adulterous relationship with another woman's husband. That is, according to Scripture, a wrong path and would undoubtedly bring disgrace to His good name.

The Shepherd tells us there will be paths and there will also be valleys (Ps. 23:3-4). We're instructed to walk through these troughs of trouble and to take our time about it. There is no question that the temptation is to run. But I have discovered that the greenest grass grows in the valleys and the most beautiful flowers bloom in the shadows! We will miss it all if we race around our problems without learning the lessons of love along the way.

The valley may well be full of shadows—valleys usually are—and some of those shadows may be foreboding, but the shadow of our Shepherd will overshadow them all. He promises us His presence. We cannot live on the mountaintops of life; valleys must be travelled. But if we know God, then we will never travel the valleys alone.

But what of the mountaintops? Sometimes we can find ourselves grappling with more problems on the heights than we find in the depths! It's easy to stay close to God when we're in trouble because we don't have too many other options. But when we are feasting after the famine is over, we may find we need the Shepherd's special help if we are going to handle the blessings He brings our way. Perhaps the oil of anointing spoken of in Psalm 23:5 is the special help God gives us to help us cope with the high points of life. He wants to help us use these blessings for His kingdom and not to build our own little empires with them. Can we be trusted with health, wealth, and happiness? How will we spend such treasures? Will we invest our "good fortune" for God? If we will, then surely our cup will overflow (Ps. 23:5).

Psalm 23 promises us that one day the Shepherd will lead us to the highest hill of all—the hill of heaven itself. What a heavenly view will meet our wondering eyes! Will heaven remind us strangely of a sheepfold? We don't know. But we do know that the most wonderful thing of all will be the permanent presence of our Lord Jesus Christ. Almost as wonderful will be the permanent absence of the old lion, Satan. As we seek to follow our Good Shepherd to that heavenly fold, He promises us that His goodness and mercy will follow us, making sure we arrive safe and sound (Ps. 23:6). Hallelujah!

•TALKING IT OVER•

1. READ AND DISCUSS.   *20 minutes*
   ☐ (The Shepherd's cross – Complete this activity
   as a whole group.)
   Psalm 22:1-21. In what ways does this passage
   describe the suffering of Christ? Be specific.

   ☐ (The Shepherd's care – Discuss in twos.)
   Ezekiel 34:2-6. In light of this passage, what
   sort of shepherd are you? Try to apply the word
   pictures in this passage personally. Ask yourself: Am I helping to nurture anyone?

   John 21:15-18. What sort of shepherd was Peter
   at this point in his life? What does this passage
   say to you?

   Psalm 23. Which aspect of the shepherd described in this psalm do you like best? Why?

2. READ, MEDITATE, AND SHARE.   *7 minutes*
   ☐ (The Shepherd's crown – Complete this exer-
   cise in twos or in small groups.)
   Psalm 24:7-10
   Hebrews 13:20-21
   1 Peter 5:4
   Meditate silently on these passages for 2 minutes; then share one thought God has given you
   about them.

3. PRAY.   *3 minutes*
   Pray sentence prayers to our Good Shepherd.

•PRAYING IT THROUGH•

Suggested Times

---

1. Read Isaiah 53:6. Make a list of "sheep" you know who are lost. Pray that these lost ones may come to know the One who bore their sins. (Use first names only if in prayer groups.)

9 minutes

---

2. Pray for sheep you know who are walking through dark valleys, that they will know God's enabling presence.

7 minutes

---

3. Pray for sheep you know who are presently on the mountaintops, that they may keep their heads about them on the heights and use their vantage points for God's glory.

7 minutes

---

4. Pray for yourself. Use a verse of Psalm 23 as you do this.

7 minutes

•DIGGING DEEPER•

1. Read Psalm 23.

2. Psalm 23:1 speaks of the Lord as a shepherd who provides everything we need. The rest of the psalm tells of a number of things the shepherd provides. Using one or two words, complete the following statements and give the verse in which each is found.

    Example: He provides me with _____rest_____ (v. 2).

    He provides me with _____ (   ).

    He provides me with _____ (   ).

    He provides me with _____ (   ).

    He provides me with _____ (   ).

    He provides me with _____ (   ).

3. In what ways does God feed *you?*

4. What are some of the "paths of righteousness" that we need to follow today?

5. The world would prefer we walk in paths of wickedness. What are some of the paths of wickedness we are tempted to follow?

6. In what ways has God comforted you recently?

7. Look up the word *comfort* in a Bible concordance. Find three verses that you think help explain comfort, and write the verses out in your own words. The following list is taken from the list of verses on comfort found in *Strong's Exhaustive Concordance of the Bible* (Abingdon).

> Gen. 5:29 - "shall comfort us concerning our work"
> Job 7:13 - "My bed shall comfort me, my couch"
> Ps. 71:21 - "and comforts me on every side."
> Isa. 22:4 - "to comfort me, because of the spoiling"
> Isa. 40:1 - "Comfort ye, comfort ye my people saith your"
> Isa. 51:3 - "the Lord shall comfort Zion"
> Isa. 61:2 - "to comfort all that mourn"
> Jer. 16:7 - "to comfort them for the dead; neither"
> Zech. 1:17 - "and the Lord shall yet comfort Zion"
> 2 Cor. 1:4 - "that we may be able to comfort them"
> 2 Cor. 2:7 - "to forgive him, and comfort him, lest"
> 1 Thes. 4:18 - "comfort one another with these words"
> 2 Thes. 2:17 - "Comfort your hearts, and stablish you"

Your paraphrase of the verses you chose on comfort:

8. Read John 10:1-18. What can we learn about Christ the Good Shepherd from this passage?

9. From that same passage, make a list of all of the things that we learn about the sheep.

10. God gives us undershepherds in the church. Read 1 Peter 5:1-4.
    Discuss the following:
    ☐ Who are the undershepherds?
    ☐ What are they to do?
    ☐ What are they not to do?
    ☐ What will their rewards be?
    ☐ What should the relationship between the undershepherds
      and the sheep be? (Cf. 1 Peter 5:5)

11. Ask yourself:
    ☐ Who am I following? What sort of shepherd is the person I'm
      following?
    ☐ Who is following me? What sort of shepherd am I?

•TOOL CHEST•
(A Suggested Optional Resource)

BIBLE CONCORDANCE
A concordance is an invaluable tool for discovering what the Bible says about any topic you choose. It lists all the biblical references to a particular word in their order of appearance in the Bible. For example, to find out what the Bible says about love, you would look up the word *love* in a concordance (the words are listed alphabetically) and read through the references listed there. The Scripture reference is given along with an excerpt of the verse that includes the word you have looked up (which is often identified by its first letter alone). Some concordances are *complete* (all the occurrences of all the most important terms, leaving out words like *the* and *and*); some are *exhaustive* (usually including even the *thes* and *ands!*); and some are simply listings of some of the major references to the most important words. The best concordances let you know in some way when the biblical writer has used different Hebrew, Aramaic, or Greek words so that you can differentiate between them. For instance, in the Bible there are numerous different words all translated by the English word *love* and they do not all have the same shade of meaning. As always, the best thing to do is to work with several different concordances for a while and see which one is best for you, before buying it. Of course, the translation you use regularly for study will influence your decision too, since each concordance is based on a particular English translation.

> Concordances to the *King James Version:*
>> Strong, J., *An Exhaustive Concordance to the Bible*
>> Young, R., *An Analytical Concordance to the Bible*
>
> Concordance for the *New International Version:*
>> Goodrick, E.W. and Kohlenberger, J.R., *The NIV Complete Concordance*
>
> Concordance for the *New American Standard Bible:*
>> Thomas, R.L., *New American Standard Exhaustive Concordance of the Bible*
>
> Concordance for the *Revised Standard Version:*
>> Ellison, J.W., *Nelson's Complete Concordance to the Revised Standard Version*

The excerpts in the Digging Deeper section of this chapter are from *Strong's Exhaustive Concordance of the Bible.* The number at the end of each reference refers you to the Hebrew and Greek dictionaries in the back of the book.

A concordance is a basic tool that should be a part of every person's study library, if possible.

selected verses from

PSALM 27

¹The Lord is my light and my salvation;
Whom shall I fear?
The Lord is the strength of my life;
Of whom shall I be afraid?

²When the wicked came against me
To eat up my flesh,
My enemies and foes,
They stumbled and fell.

³Though an army should encamp against me,
My heart shall not fear;
Though war should rise against me,
In this I will be confident.

⁴One thing I have desired of the Lord,
That will I seek:
That I may dwell in the house of the Lord
All the days of my life,
To behold the beauty of the Lord,
And to inquire in His temple.

⁵For in the time of trouble
He shall hide me in His pavilion;
In the secret place of His tabernacle
He shall hide me;
He shall set me high upon a rock.

. . . .

⁷Hear, O Lord, when I cry with my voice!
Have mercy also upon me, and answer me.

⁸When You said, "Seek My face,"
My heart said to You,
"Your face, Lord, I will seek."

⁹Do not hide Your face from me;
Do not turn Your servant away in anger;
You have been my help;
Do not leave me nor forsake me,
O God of my salvation.

¹⁰When my father and my mother forsake me;
Then the Lord will take care of me.

. . . .

¹⁴Wait on the Lord;
Be of good courage,
And He shall strengthen your heart;
Wait, I say, on the Lord!

4

TheLordMyLight

•FOOD FOR THOUGHT•

God is the source of light. "And God said, 'Let there be light,' and there was light. God saw that the light was good" (Gen. 1:3). The very atmosphere of heaven is light. There is no night there, and the Lamb is the lamp of it (Rev. 21:23). When the Apostle John was on the Isle of Patmos, he saw the risen Lamb of God and said, "His face was like the sun shining in all its brilliance" (Rev. 1:16). The force of that Light is such, that meeting it men fall on their faces to the earth. Look at Saul on the Damascus road: "As he [Saul] neared Damascus on his journey, suddenly a light from heaven flashed around him. He fell to the ground and heard a voice say to him, 'Saul, Saul, why do you persecute me?' " (Acts 9:3) Once a man has seen the Light of life and has received that Light, he then becomes a lightbearer. It was said of John the Baptist, "John was a lamp that burned and gave light" (John 5:35). He illuminated the Lamb of God so that others could follow Him. Jesus said, "I am the Light of the world" (John 8:12). He also said, "You are the light of the world" (Matt. 5:14).

Light begets life—physically and materially we see that force operating in creation. It is also true in the spiritual realm. In Scripture we read about the sons of light and the sons of darkness (Eph. 5:8-14; 1 Thes. 5:5). The sons of darkness refuse to come to the light because they want to keep their doings secret, and they know that light tells secrets (John 3:20). Sons of light, on the other hand, are to live in the light. Once they have been enlightened by the Holy Spirit, they have no right to live as sons of darkness anymore. Yet, if the truth be told, this is often what happens. Christians can know the Christ who is their light, and yet skulk about in dark places fearing exposure because they are ashamed of their behavior. We can be afraid of God and afraid of the darkness in our lives at the same time. David knew all about this and that is why he penned the 27th Psalm.

There were plenty of dark circumstances surrounding King David. There was the darkness of danger, of war, even of death itself. Then there was the darkness of the fear of the future. Perhaps this was the greatest darkness of all. When Job's life fell apart after many years of health, wealth, and happiness, he said, "What I feared has come upon me; what I dreaded has happened to me" (Job 3:25). He had been living in the light of the good life and yet had experienced within his heart the dark fear of things that *might* happen to him in the future.

Haven't you experienced such fears? I have. When my children were small, I feared they would never grow up. When I got engaged, I feared I would never make the wedding day. When I did make it to the altar, I began to fear we would never have children. When we did have children, I feared they would never grow up, get married, have children, and on and on and on. There is only so much of life you can control. None of us can control outward circumstances. David, fearing such hostile intervention in his life, said, "The Lord is my light and my salvation—whom shall I fear? The Lord is the stronghold of my life—of whom shall I be afraid?" (Ps. 27:1)

David also battled with inner conflicts. Spiritually, the light inside his heart appeared to flicker and threatened to go out. God's face seemed vailed—the light dim. Had God turned away from him in his time of need? There is no greater darkness than that of the fear we are forsaken by God. "Do not hide Your face from me, do not turn Your servant away in anger; You have been my helper. Do not reject me or forsake me, O God my Saviour" (Ps. 27:9).

"Will God leave us?" we agonize. Perhaps we have sinned as believers. We have lived as children of darkness rather than as children of light. Is God angry? Another way to translate verse 9 might be, "My heart said unto Thee, 'Let my face seek Thy face!' " Oh, to be face to face again after we have turned our backs to the light of life!

This reminds me of an incident in the life of David and Absalom, his son. Absalom had murdered his brother, Amnon, because he had defiled their sister, Tamar. After the murder, Absalom fled because King David was furious and mourned for Amnon. After three years in exile, Absalom managed to return to Jerusalem but was told by the king, "He must go to his own house; he must not see my face" (2 Sam. 14:24). This state of affairs continued for two years. Absalom could not bear his punishment, and sent Joab to King David saying, " 'Why have I come from Geshur? It would be better for me if I were still there! Now then, I want to see the king's face, and if I am guilty of anything, let him put me to death' " (2 Sam. 14:32). So father and son were reconciled.

If only we would care as much as Absalom cared. If we fear God's face is hidden because we have displeased Him, and yet ask Him to look toward us again, no matter what sort of rebellious children we have been, how much more gracious and loving will God our heavenly King be than the earthly King David? He will permit us to see His face again and we will find, as John did on Patmos, "His face was like the sun shining in all its brilliance" (Rev. 1:16).

Add to the dark circumstances surrounding King David, the spiritual conflict within his own heart and the rejection he may have felt from his own family—the outlook began to look very black indeed. In Psalm 27:10 David talks about his father and mother forsaking him. What deep darkness that is! As a child, David appears to have had little relationship with his parents; he was always being left out. When Samuel came to town, all of David's brothers—but not David—were invited to meet the great judge (1 Sam. 16:5-11). Then David's brothers scolded him as if he were a mischievous child when he arrived at the battlefield to greet them (1 Sam. 17:28-30).

It's tough when your family rejects you. Perhaps you have become a Christian and have tried to share the excitement of your newfound faith with those closest to you. But it hasn't worked. Instead, you've been met with, "What do you know?" or "You are the youngest!" David, in experiencing this kind of darkness, said, "Though my father and mother forsake me, the Lord will receive me" (Ps. 27:10). The One who is the light of our lives will lift us into a light place despite the darkness of our relationships.

The secret of survival, yea revival, in such circumstances is found in verse 14—"Wait for the Lord; be strong and take heart and wait for the Lord" (Ps. 27:14). We need to turn our faces toward the Lord, expecting that His face will indeed be turned toward us in forgiveness and encouragement. We can have a joyful hope; He will lighten our darkness and strengthen our hearts.

Worship dispels fear. There is an inner sanctuary of security and serenity called praise that hides our frightened spirits from all dark fears, even as a mother hides the face of her child from a terrible accident.

Next time fear and darkness roll over you, lift up your head and sing as David sang, "The Lord is my light and my salvation—whom shall I fear? The Lord is the stronghold of my life—of whom shall I be afraid?" (Ps. 27:1)

•TALKING IT OVER•

Suggested Times

---

1. PARAPHRASE AND DISCUSS.   *7 minutes*
Choose a verse from the list of references below
and put it in your own words. What does it say to
you personally?

John 1:5	John 3:19	John 3:20-21
John 12:46	John 5:35	Ephesians 5:8
Revelation 21:23	1 John 1:7	1 John 2:9-10

---

2. SHARE PERSONALLY.   *7 minutes*
Discuss these questions as a group:
   ☐ What was one of your worst childhood fears?
   ☐ What is one of your worst fears now?

---

3. READ AND DISCUSS.   *11 minutes*
Work on this exercise in twos initially. Then share
what you find with the rest of the group.

   ☐ Choose *one* passage from the list below and read
   it. As you read, look for an answer to this
   question: What do you learn of God that helps
   you see that He is bigger than your fears?

Genesis 11:8	Luke 9:12-17
1 Kings 19:1-7	John 11:38-44
Isaiah 61:8	John 20:19-23

   ☐ Read Romans 8:28. Then discuss these questions: What do you think this verse implies?
   How can we see God's goodness in *all* things
   when some situations are so bad?

---

4. APPLY TO LIFE.   *5 minutes*
Write down in a sentence one step of action you
need to take this week to deal with one of your
fears. When and what will it be?

•PRAYING IT THROUGH•

Suggested Times

1. Read the account of John's vision of Christ in Revelation 1:12-16. Spend 5 minutes praising God for the Lord Jesus as you've seen Him through the eyes of the Apostle John.

10 minutes

2. Pray for any "sons of darkness" you know who need to see the Light of life.

5 minutes

3. Pray for Christians you know whose lives are being lived in the darkness of fear.

5 minutes

4. Meditate for 2 minutes on 1 John 1:5-10. Then choose a verse from this passage and pray it for yourself.

5 minutes

•DIGGING DEEPER•

1. Read Psalm 27.

2. Outline Psalm 27 by giving a title to each group of verses listed. (NOTE: Verse groupings are taken from the *New International Version.*)

   (vv. 1-3)

   (vv. 4-6)

   (vv. 7-12)

   (vv. 13-14)

3. How do we tend to react when "evil men" advance against us or when "enemies" attack us?

4. According to verses 2-3 of Psalm 27, how should we react and why?

5. What do we learn about God from verses 4-6?

6. What should be our response to what we learned about God, according to verse 6?

7. Reread Psalm 27:7-12. When we pray as David did in these verses, what assurance do we have that God hears us? For added insight into the answer to that question, look up the following verses:

Joshua 1:5

Psalm 27:5

Psalm 91:4

Isaiah 25:4

Isaiah 43:2

Matthew 18:20

Matthew 28:20

Luke 21:18

James 4:8

1 Peter 5:7

8. About what is David confident? (vv. 13-14)

9. What do you think we should do while we are "waiting" (Ps. 27:14) for the Lord?

10. What is something you fear for the future and how are you dealing with that fear?

11. The encyclopedic entry for "fear" in *The Zondervan Pictorial Encyclopedia of the Bible* (volume 2, Merrill C. Tenney, editor, pp. 519-520) talks about two kinds of fear—fear of God and fear of evil. Included in the explanation is a paragraph on "banishing fear—freedom from fear."

Banishing fear—freedom from fear
By precept and example Jesus taught His disciples to make conquest of their fears. It can be done.
By the presence of God. David said triumphantly, "I will fear no evil; for Thou art with me" (Ps. 23:4b). Long before this, God had said to Abraham, "Fear not, Abram, I

am your shield" (Gen. 15:1). To Isaiah He said for Israel, "Fear not, for I have redeemed you. . . . Fear not, for I am with you" (Isa. 43:1, 5). Divine visible presence, after the first startling moments, always dispelled fears (Ex. 3:6; Matt. 12:27; 17:6ff; Luke 1:30; 2:10). Moreover, God's unseen presence hovers over His own and protects them. Elisha had at his command a mountain covered with "horses and chariots of fire" (2 Kings 6:17). And Jesus had in reserve "more than twelve legions of angels" (Matt. 26:53).

By perfected love. "The fear of God" in the OT yielded to "the love of God" in the NT. Though the awesome nature of God will never diminish, His fatherly love was manifested through Jesus. His tenderness has replaced terror. Consequently, John could give the Christian antidote for fear: "There is no fear in love; but perfect love casts out fear. For fear has to do with punishment, and he who fears has not been perfected in love" (1 John 4:18). The Christian should have no fear of hunger, nakedness, sickness, suffering, wicked people, death, nor judgment. All have lost their power of fear in the love of Christ. "Fear not, little flock, for it is your Father's good pleasure to give you the kingdom" (Luke 12:32).

Now, in your own words write a sentence or two about how to deal with fear.

•TOOL CHEST•
(A Suggested Optional Resource)

BIBLE ENCYCLOPEDIAS

Bible encyclopedias are multivolume sets of articles about people, places, and subjects arranged in alphabetical order (like a Bible dictionary). These articles go into much greater detail than a Bible dictionary, however. They contain historical background information and sometimes function even as commentaries on the biblical books. Much helpful information is available in this type of Bible study tool. It is a great source to turn to and can save a lot of time and effort.

These sets, however, can be expensive—$100 or more—because they contain several volumes. *The Zondervan Pictorial Encyclopedia of the Bible*, edited by Merrill C. Tenney (Zondervan, 1975, 1976) is a five-volume set. Because of the great cost, it is unlikely that an individual would invest in one of these sets early on in the acquisition of a study library. However, a church could add a set to the church library, or a group of people could invest in a set together. They may also be available at a public library or university library.

A Bible encyclopedia is easy to use. Simply look up the name, place, or subject you are interested in, and *read!*

PSALM 51

¹Have mercy upon me, O God,
  According to Your lovingkindness;
According to the multitude of Your tender mercies,
  Blot out my transgressions.

. . . .

³For I acknowledge my transgressions,
  And my sin is ever before me.

⁴Against You, You only, have I sinned,
  And done this evil in Your sight—
That You may be found just when You speak,
  And blameless when You judge.

. . . .

⁷Purge me with hyssop, and I shall be clean;
  Wash me, and I shall be whiter than snow.

⁸Make me to hear joy and gladness,
  That the bones which You have broken may rejoice.

. . . .

¹⁰Create in me a clean heart, O God,
  And renew a steadfast spirit within me.

¹¹Do not cast me away from Your presence,
  And do not take Your Holy Spirit from me.

¹²Restore to me the joy of Your salvation,
  And uphold me with Your generous Spirit.

¹³Then I will teach transgressors Your ways,
  And sinners shall be converted to You.

¹⁴Deliver me from bloodguiltiness, O God,
  The God of my salvation,
  And my tongue shall sing aloud of Your
    righteousness.

¹⁵O LORD, open my lips,
  And my mouth shall show forth Your praise.

¹⁶For You do not desire sacrifice,
  or else I would give it;
You do not delight in burnt offering.

¹⁷The sacrifices of God are a broken spirit,
  A broken and a contrite heart—
These, O God, You will not despise.

. . . .

5

The Lord My Forgiveness

•FOOD FOR THOUGHT•

Failure is never final for the believer! David found that out and wrote a psalm about it.

First Corinthians 10:6 tells us that "these things [that happened to the children of Israel] became our examples, to the intent that we should not lust after evil things as they also lusted." The Word of God not only records the good in people's characters, it also exposes the bad so that we can better deal with our own shortcomings and temptations and know how to handle them.

First, temptation is not sin, otherwise Jesus could be called a sinner because He was tempted (Matt. 4:1-11). An old Chinese proverb says, "You can't stop the birds from flying over your head, but you *can* keep them from nesting in your hair!" We may not be able to prevent evil thoughts from entering our minds, but we can stop them from settling in and setting up house in our thinking!

Second, God has promised to be with us in temptation and see us through it: "No temptation has overtaken you except such as is common to man; but God is faithful, who will not allow you to be tempted beyond what you are able, but with the temptation will also make the way of escape, that you may be able to bear it" (1 Cor. 10:13). This verse does *not* promise to deliver us *out* of the fiery furnace of adversity without first having delivered us *in* it!

In Daniel's day, Shadrach, Meshach, and Abednego were thrown into a white hot furnace. As King Nebuchadnezzar and his counselors stood by to watch their demise, they were astounded to see *four* men walking around in the flames unsinged. "Didn't we throw only three men to their deaths?" they wondered. What's more, the prisoners appeared to be fit and well and very excited to have with them the fourth man who had apparently appeared from nowhere! Of course *we* know who the mystery man was, don't we? It was the Lord Jesus

63

Christ (Dan. 3:25) who had come to deliver His faithful servants in the very midst of their trouble. This particular incident tells me that Jesus Christ will be all that I need, no matter how "hot" a spot I find myself in. He will not allow me to *burn up* or *burn out*, but rather will enable me to *burn on* brightly in my witness for Him.

A third thing to remember about temptation is that it is universal. It confronts the best as well as the worst of us. Most of us know this to be true, and yet something inside us finds it hard to accept the reality that "good people" *are* tempted and that some of the "best people" succumb to temptation. "Commoners, not kings, will be the ones who fail to repulse Satan's attacks," we tell ourselves. And yet David, whom Scripture calls "a man after God's own heart," failed to rebuff the tempter and committed adultery with the wife of one of his most trusted friends. Adding sin to sin, David arranged to have this friend—Uriah—killed in order to cover up his own sin. It took God's rebuke through the Prophet Nathan to bring David to his knees in repentance (2 Sam. 12:20)—almost a whole year after the incident!

What can we learn from David's experience? We must learn to recognize temptation in whatever form it comes to us. Lucifer is not stupid—he did not offer Eve a rotten apple! Too, we must recognize that we are capable of anything. Do we know ourselves that well?

After sharing these thoughts with some ladies in Australia, a young woman approached me and said, "I can imagine myself battering my child (she had four infants under six!), but not committing adultery. I would *never* do that!"

"That's a dangerous statement to make," I replied. "Never say never!"

I asked her if she had ever had the chance to be unfaithful. She replied honestly enough, "Yes, and it was very easy for me to resist."

"Did the temptation come in the shape of a King David or a King Lear?" I inquired next.

"A King Lear" she replied, grinning. She got the point. All of us find it comparatively simple to refuse the advances of a Lear but what about a David? Do we really know how we would react if we were the object of the attentions of such a charming man?

A fourth point to be made relates to the timing of temptation. The devil always bides his time. He was content to wait until David had grown to be middle-aged. The king lay in bed till late one evening. He felt restless. Perhaps seeking the cooler breezes of the early evening, the king walked out on the roof of his house. There he saw a very beautiful woman taking a bath. The woman's husband had been out of town for quite some time. Laziness added to loneliness resulted in a combustible mix for David and Bathsheba. If people don't know themselves well, watch themselves carefully, and keep themselves from acting out their feelings, an incredible mess can ensue! "But how," you ask, "*do* we keep from yielding to temptation?"

First, we need to realize that God holds us fully responsible for our own actions—for our responses to the tempter. Knowing that should help us do the right thing even when everyone else is doing the wrong thing. When Nathan finally confronted David about his sin, David did not make excuses. He didn't say, "It's all my dad's fault—he never paid any attention to me as a kid! He was forever showing my brothers favoritism and leaving me out in the fields with the sheep." And he didn't say, "It was all Bathsheba's fault," though he could quite legitimately have complained about her taking her bath in full view of his veranda instead of in the privacy of her bedroom. Rather, David said, "I have sinned." He acknowledged that there was no one to blame but himself. That's not to say that Bathsheba was exempt—of course she was guilty too—but we stand before God on our own and must answer for our own actions. When faced with God's knowledge of our sin, we have a choice to make: We can argue our case, or we can confess our sins as David did and be restored to fellowship with Him.

If we find it difficult to find the right words, we can borrow David's from Psalm 51 and make them our own. We can start by agreeing with God that we have sinned against Him (51:3-4), for any sin against man is a sin against God. It took David a long time to confess his sinful actions. No doubt he felt guilty, but one can learn to live with guilt, and David had lived with his guilt for so long, he failed to remember what it was like to live without it. Eventually David faced up to the reality that the Lord was displeased with him. He realized it had been a long, long time since he had had a song to sing. (You see, guilt doesn't know any songs! Guilt is being inwardly angry with yourself for doing something you know very well is quite wrong. And angry people generally don't make very good composers.) Having confessed his sin, David prayed about the guilt of it.

Have you ever admitted your sin, confessed it, believed God has heard you and forgiven you, and yet continued to feel guilty about it? David had to learn to forgive himself. After all, God had forgiven him. And what God forgives and forgets, we have no right to remember (Ps. 103:12). With David, we need to pray, "Create in me a pure heart, O God. . . . Save me from bloodguilt" (Ps. 51:10, 14).

One of my favorite hymns speaks to this point. It talks of a *full* salvation that cleanses the soul *and* mends the mind of those merciless memories that stand as silent accusers in our hearts, pointing their fingers at past demeanors.

> Full salvation! Full salvation!
>   Lo, the fountain opened wide,
> Streams through every land and nation
>   From the Saviour's wounded side.
>   Full salvation!
> Streams an endless crimson tide.
>
> Love's resistless current sweeping
>   All the regions deep within;
> Thought, and wish, and senses keeping
>   Now, and every instant, clean:
>   Full salvation!
> From the guilt and power of sin.

We have to believe that God has cast our sins into the depths of the sea and has erected a warning sign over them that says NO DREDGING!

Once God has dealt with our sins as well as the guilt of them, we will find ourselves free to pray as David prayed, "O Lord, open my lips, and my mouth shall show forth Your praise" (51:15). God had to cleanse David's lips before He could use them again—and He did. David came to believe he was very special, though deeply fallen. God let David know he was still greatly loved, and that wondrous fact enabled the king to recommit his life to the service of Jehovah.

God also restored David's joy. Sin is a terrible "killjoy"—no matter who would have us believe otherwise. When I was debating whether or not I should become a Christian, I was plagued with the thought that if I did become a Christian I would never smile again! Where do such morose meditations come from? From whom else but the one who has had nothing to smile about since he was cast out of the abode of happiness—Satan himself! He, being the father of lies, would have us believe that being "good" is a very long-faced affair. It goes without saying that I've discovered quite the opposite to be true!

After David was restored and forgiven, God allowed him to continue ministering even though he would never again enjoy as fully the godly influence he had once exercised in Israel. (Even his children despised and rose up against him.) God save us from the repercussions of our sinful stupidity! Make no mistake—if we fall to temptation, we may, like David, end up forfeiting certain privileges of leadership and influence. David's testimony had been terribly marred, but God, in His grace, still had work for David to do. It's not how we begin the Christian life that really matters, it's how we finish it that's important. But if we, like David, really "blow it," we need to know we have a resource in God. Forgiveness is available.

We learn in 2 Samuel 12:18 that David and Bathsheba's baby died. But God in His goodness granted to the grieving couple a new son (2 Sam. 12:24). Now isn't *that* just like God? Failure, after all, is never final for the believer—and He wants us to know it!

•TALKING IT OVER•

1. READ AND DISCUSS.   *15 minutes*
   ☐ Read together Luke 4:1-13. Then discuss these
   questions: How was David's temptation similar
   to our Lord's? What *did* Jesus do that David
   didn't? Is temptation sin?

   ☐ After reading Psalm 51:3-13 and 1 John 1:5-10,
   briefly review the steps to repentance mentioned in these two passages.

2. INTERPRET PERSONALLY.   *10 minutes*
   Choose one of the following references and say
   what the verses mean to you.

   | A *new start* | A *new spirit* | A *new steadfastness* |
   | Ps. 51:10 | Ps. 51:11, 17 | Psa. 51:10 |

   | A *new song* | A *new service* | A *new son* |
   | Ps. 51:12, 15 | Ps. 51:13 | 2 Sam. 12:24-25 |

3. PRAY.   *5 minutes*
   Using Psalm 51 as a basis, pray prayers
   of repentance.

•PRAYING IT THROUGH•

Suggested Times

---

1. Praise God for Christians in society today who occupy privileged and visible positions. Pray for their protection. Pray too that God would keep them from yielding to temptation.

   5 minutes

---

2. Read Ephesians 5:22-33. Then pray for Christian counselors and for Christian marriages using this passage.

   10 minutes

---

3. Pray silently for your family and for yourself.

   5 minutes

•DIGGING DEEPER•

1. Read Psalm 51 in two different Bible translations.

2. Divide the psalm into four or five main sections and come up with a title for each section.

   (vv.   ) _____

   (vv.   ) _____

   (vv.   ) _____

   (vv.   ) _____

   (vv.   ) _____

3. Read 2 Samuel 11–12.

4. According to 2 Samuel 11, how did David get into the situation that is spoken of in Psalm 51? What would be a parallel situation today?

5. Drawing from the Prophet Nathan's conversation with David in 2 Samuel 12, what were David's sins?

6. What did God feel about David's sin?

7. What do *you* feel about what God felt?

8. How do you think David felt (Ps. 51:1-5)?

9. In what way is God's conviction of sin a sign of His love? (See Hebrews 12:6-7.)

10. Briefly describe a time when you sinned and you felt the conviction of God.

11. What does David ask for in Psalm 51:10-12?

12. Note how in verse 11, David asks God not to take His Holy Spirit from him. One aspect of the Holy Spirit's work in our lives is to convict us of all ungodliness.

For added insight into the presence and work of the Hoy Spirit in the Old Testament, read the following excerpt from the *Evangelical Dictionary of Theology* (Baker, pp. 521-522).

The phrase "Holy Spirit" appears in two contexts in the

OT, but is qualified both times as God's holy Spirit (Ps. 51:11; Isa. 63:10-11, 14), such that it is clear that God himself is the referent, not *the* Holy Spirit which is encountered in the NT. The OT does not contain an idea of a semi-independent divine entity, the Holy Spirit. Rather, we find special expressions of God's activity with and through men. God's spirit is holy in the same way His word and His name are holy; they are all forms of his revelation and, as such, are set in antithesis to all things human or material. The OT, especially the prophets, anticipates a time when God, who is holy (or "other than/separate from" men; cf. Hosea 11:9) will pour out his spirit on men (Joel 2:28ff.; Isa. 11:1ff.; Ezek. 36:14ff.), who will themselves become holy. The Messiah/Servant of God will be the one upon whom the spirit rests (Isa. 11:1ff.; 42:1ff.; 63:1ff.), and will inaugurate the time of salvation (Ezek. 36:14ff.; cf. Jer. 31:31ff.).

13. On your own, read through the Scripture references listed in the *Dictionary* excerpt above.

14. Why do you think David says that the sacrifices of God are a broken and contrite heart?

15. How can you help those who have been involved in sin to come to repentance and be cleansed, without appearing "holier than thou"?

•TOOL CHEST•
(A Suggested Optional Resource)

THEOLOGICAL DICTIONARY
The *Evangelical Dictionary of Theology,* edited by Walter A. Elwell (Baker, 1984) is the Bible study tool highlighted in this chapter's Digging Deeper section. A dictionary of theology is similar to a Bible dictionary in that it provides notes on how a word or subject is used in both the Old and New Testaments. However, in addition to that information, a theological dictionary also has comments on how the *topic* has been viewed by the church down through the years. The topics are listed in alphabetical order.

In 1985, this 1,200-page dictionary won the Publisher of the Year award in *Eternity* magazine's 27th Book of the Year poll.

PSALM 119

. . . .

[86]All Your commandments are faithful;
  They persecute me wrongfully;
    Help me!

[87]They almost made an end of me on earth,
    But I did not forsake Your precepts.

[88]Revive me according to Your lovingkindness,
    So that I may keep the testimony of Your mouth.

. . . .

[97]Oh, how I love Your law!
  It is my meditation all the day.

[98]You, through Your commandments,
    make me wiser than my enemies;
  For they are ever with me.

[99]I have more understanding than all my teachers,
    For Your testimonies are my meditation.

[100]I understand more than the ancients,
  Because I keep Your precepts.

[101]I have restrained my feet from every evil way,
    That I may keep Your Word.

[102]I have not departed from Your judgments,
    For You Yourself have taught me.

[103]How sweet are Your words to my taste,
    Sweeter than honey to my mouth!

[104]Through Your precepts I get understanding;
    Therefore I hate every false way.

. . . .

[129]Your testimonies are wonderful;
  Therefore my soul keeps them.

[130]The entrance of Your words gives light;
    It gives understanding to the simple.

. . . .

[152]Concerning Your testimonies, I have known of old
    That You have founded them forever.

. . . .

[174]I long for Your salvation, O LORD,
  And Your law is my delight.

[175]Let my soul live, and it shall praise You;
    And let Your judgments help me.

6

The Lord My Word

•FOOD FOR THOUGHT•

No man goes to heaven unless he knows God. Scripture tells us that knowing God is imperative for salvation: "And this is the testimony: that God has given us eternal life, and this life is in His Son. He who has the Son has life" (1 John 5:11-12a). God *can* be known. Now that's good news!

Shortly after our family immigrated to the United States, I turned on my car radio just in time to hear the announcer say, "Stay tuned for total information news."

"That's good," I thought as I settled down to listen to what I thought would be a good hour of world events. I was startled, however, to hear five minutes of headline news instead—all of it having to do with the United States or relating to it. I quickly realized that "total information news" did not necessarily mean an exhaustive coverage of world happenings; rather, it meant giving minimum facts about the most important incidents. Similarly, we need not know everything about the Almighty before we can have eternal life. God has made sure that man can obtain a knowledge of Him that is totally adequate for meeting his need of eternal salvation. The Bible, if you like, contains God's headline news. It will take eternity to learn everything else there is to know about the King and His kingdom.

God's revelation of Himself is not only adequate, it is progressive. Psalm 119:90-91 tells us, "Your faithfulness continues through all generations; You established the earth, and it endures. Your laws endure to this day, for all things serve You." Nature reveals the glory of God to man. In fact, in Romans 1:20 we learn that man is without excuse if he says he has not "seen" God in nature. God has revealed enough of His power and glory in the marvelous things He has made to lead men to worship Him.

But God did not leave the revelation of Himself strictly to nature.

He put a witness deep down inside every one of us, in the human conscience. The conscience works like an early warning system, giving us inner, moral knowledge. A scriptural precept gives the details of that morality, explaining to man his obligation as enjoined by God. In Psalm 119:104 the psalmist says, "I gain understanding from Your precepts; therefore I hate every wrong path." And the writer to the Hebrews adds that God has promised to "put My laws in their hearts . . . [and] write them on their minds" (Heb. 10:16).

Besides revealing Himself in creation and conscience, God has given us something even more concrete—His written Word. Lest we be left wondering just what was right and what was wrong, He wrote down on tablets of stone ten fundamental principles for life. These are the princples on which He intends we should craft our behavior. Exodus 24:12 says, "I will give you the tablets of stone, with the law and commands I have written." I'm sure you will agree that this was a pretty substantial message God gave the human race. These fundamental principles have to do with our relationship with God, with other people, and with ourselves. Western society is based on these ten commandments. They are not ten ammendments or suggestions, but rather God's legal pronouncements and rules of divine administration that we ignore at our peril.

God's clear Self-revelation is contained in two parts of one book. The two parts are complimentary. "The new is in the old revealed; the old is in the new concealed." We can sum it up this way: The Old Testament is preparation; the Gospels, manifestation; the Acts of the Apostles, propagation; the Epistles, explanation; and the revelation of John, consummation. God in Christ intervened in human history. The Old Testament set the stage for it; the New Testament describes it.

There is no other portion of Scripture that deals more explicitly with God's Self-revelation than Psalm 119. It is here that we are told His Word is relevant forever (v. 152), that its testimonies are wonderful (v. 129), and that on entering our lives, that Word will give our darkened souls spiritual enlightenment (v. 130).

Of all the ways God shows Himself to us, the Word of God is by far the most trustworthy of His revelations. After all, nature is spoiled because of sin and man has learned to chloroform his human conscience to the degree that he can no longer determine what is truth and what is error. Psalm 119:86 assures us, "All Your commands are trustworthy."

The Bible testifies to its own integrity and claims to be the Word of life (Phil. 2:16), of truth (Eph. 1:13), of salvation (Acts 13:26), and of reconciliation (2 Cor. 5:19).

"But," some may ask, "how can we be absolutely sure that what we have between the covers of our Bibles are the original words?" Have you ever played the game where one person whispers a sentence to the person next to him and so on and so forth down the line? This game illustrates how distorted a message can become when passed along from one person to another. How can we be sure the same thing has not happened to God's words as they were shared down through the centuries?

It is very exciting to discover that though the original texts of the Bible have all been lost, we have in the British and Vatican museums the most ancient copies made from the originals. Great translations have been produced from these copies and are available to us in our own language. Eminent scholars versed in biblical knowledge have helped to confirm data, and science has become a friend, confirming many of the statements of Scripture. Seeming contradictions have turned out to be "difficulties" and not "errors." Most of these problems have been resolved.

A young man once told me that he thought the four Gospels were full of contradictions. "Why," he said, "one writer tells a story the others omit altogether, and when all four Gospel authors describe the same event, they often differ." I explained to the young man that the very differences underscore the authenticity of the Word of God. I went on to explain, "It is like four men going to watch a football game, coming home, and writing their eyewitness accounts of the game. Obviously, each one will record in a similar way the basic facts, such as, who won, who kicked the field goals, etc. But many of the other facts that are included in the individual accounts will be determined by the things that interest the different writers, and that in turn will be determined by their own backgrounds and cultures."

The writers of Scripture were inspired by God (2 Tim. 3:16). Christ endorsed the Old Testament (Matt. 4:4), and told us how important it is that we know the Scriptures so we can be delivered from error (Matt. 22:29). I would humbly add my own personal affirmation of Holy Writ by saying that "[His] decrees are the theme of my song wherever I lodge" (Psa. 119:54) and that "If [His] law had not been my delight, I would have perished in my affliction" (Ps. 119:92). By the time we leave the Old Testament Scriptures and turn to the New Testament where we see God revealed in Jesus Christ (John 1:1), we can already be armed with the knowledge we need to know God for ourselves.

"But what about people who refuse to read the Bible for one

reason or another," you ask, "how will they ever see God?" The Apostle Paul tells us *we* can help them. Having become partakers of His divine nature by receiving His Holy Spirit, we will be "living epistles," known and read of all men (2 Cor. 3:2). It reminds me of a German teenager who once testified at a youth camp, saying, "I am 'ze' Bible on two legs!" We may be the only Bible that some people will ever read. What a challenge! And what a privilege.

•TALKING IT OVER•

1. REVIEW AND DISCUSS.   *10 minutes*
   Review ways in which God has revealed Himself
   to us. Choose a verse from the list which follows
   and discuss it with one other person in the group.
   You may need to read the verses preceding and
   following the verses you select to help you put it in
   context.

Ex. 24:12	Ps. 119:86	Ps. 119:89-90
John 1:14	2 Cor. 3:2-3	Heb. 10:16

2. READ AND SHARE.   *10 minutes*
   Look up as many of the following verses as you can
   and tell which picture means the most to you and
   why.

Lamp	Psalm 119:105
Fire/hammer	Jeremiah 23:29
Sword	Ephesians 6:17
Milk	1 Peter 2:2
Gold/honey	Psalm 19:10
Seed	Luke 8:11

3. READ AND APPLY.   *10 minutes*
   ☐ Psalm 119 is marked out in sections. Choose
   one section of this psalm and read it silently.
   Then share with the group one verse in that
   section that speaks clearly to you something
   about the Word of God.

   ☐ Read 2 Timothy 2:16 in as many different
   translations as are available in your group. Answer this: Which part of this verse is a challenge? a rebuke? an encouragement?

•PRAYING IT THROUGH•

1. Praise God for: *5 minutes*
   □ The resources we have in our culture to know His Word.
   □ The people in our lives who have taught us that saving Word (i.e., Sunday School teachers, parents, pastors, etc.).

2. Pray for: *10 minutes*
   □ The work of the Gideons who place Bibles in hotels, schools, hospitals, etc.
   □ Wycliffe Bible translators and other organizations that are committed to putting God's Word in other languages. Pray that they would have the funds they need to continue their work and that they would be encouraged in their service.
   □ People around the world who only have part of the Scriptures in their own language.
   □ People who live in countries where they are forbidden to read the Bible.

3. Pray for yourself: *5 minutes*
   □ That you would not take for granted the blessing of having God's Word.
   □ That you would not be lazy in your study of the Word of God.

•DIGGING DEEPER•

1. Skim Psalm 119. One topic is mentioned over and over again. What topic is it?

2. Background information on Psalm 119, taken from *Eerdman's Handbook of the Bible*.

   This is the longest psalm of all—and the most formal and elaborate in concept. There are 22 eight-verse sections. Each section begins with a successive letter of the Hebrew alphabet, and each verse within the section begins with the same letter. Within this stylized pattern the psalmist makes a series of individual, though not isolated or disconnected, statements about the "law" (God's teaching) and the individual—interspersed with frequent prayers. He uses ten different words to describe it: God's law, His testimonies (instruction), precepts, statutes, commandments, ordinances (decrees), word, ways (paths), promises, and judgments (rulings). And one or other of these descriptions occurs in all but a very few verses. He seems to have taken the same delight in the discipline set by this complex poetic form, as he did in the study of the law itself" (*Eerdmans*, p. 350).

3. How do these verses of Psalm 119 describe the Word of God?

   v. 4

   v. 28

   v. 30

   v. 39

   v. 52

   v. 62

   v. 86

v. 93

v. 96

v. 98

v. 111

v. 129

v. 141

v. 152

4. According to verses 1 and 2 of Psalm 119, how does a person become blessed?

5. How would you summarize the psalmist's desire in verses 1-16?

6. How does the psalmist pursue an understanding of the Word of God in verses 9-16?

7. What five things does the psalmist ask for in verses 33-37?

8. What is the reaction of the psalmist when God's Law is not obeyed? (See verses 53 and 136.)

9. Read Romans 13:9-10. Summarize what Paul teaches about the Law. How can we fulfill those demands?

10. Read Psalm 119:10, 20, 55, 62, 97, 147-148, 164. How does your eagerness to learn God's Word compare with that of the psalmist?

11. If you feel you need to put more emphasis on learning the Word of God, what will you do this week to change what you're doing?

•TOOL CHEST•
(A Suggested Optional Resource)

BIBLE HANDBOOK

A Bible handbook is similar to a Bible dictionary; the main difference is that a Bible dictionary has short articles arranged alphabetically, while a Bible handbook provides a brief running commentary of each of the books of the Bible. Many handbooks, such as *Eerdman's Handbook to the Bible*, also contain articles about the Bible—how to use the Bible; historical background about the times, the authors, and the culture; and main themes in the Bible. *Eerdman's Handbook* also contains tables of miracles and parables in the Bible, a "who's who," and a list of subjects and events. It is lavishly illustrated with photographs, drawings, and charts, and is easy to understand, so that it would be suitable for use as a family devotional tool.

PSALM 137

[1]By the rivers of Babylon,
    There we sat down, yea, we wept
When we remembered Zion.

[2]We hung our harps
Upon the willows in the midst of it.

[3]For there those who carried us away
    captive required of us a song,
And those who plundered us required
    of us mirth,
Saying, "Sing us one of the songs of
    Zion!"

[4]How shall we sing the LORD's song
In a foreign land?

[5]If I forget you, O Jerusalem,
Let my right hand forget her skill!

[6]If I do not remember you,
Let my tongue cling to the roof of my
    mouth—
If I do not exalt Jerusalem
Above my chief joy.

[7]Remember, O LORD, against the sons
    of Edom
The day of Jerusalem,
Who said, "Raze it, raze it,
To its very foundation!"

[8]O daughter of Babylon,
    who are to be destroyed,
Happy shall he be who repays you as
    you have served us!

[9]Happy shall he be who takes and
    dashes
Your little ones against the rock.

7

The Lord My Song

•FOOD FOR THOUGHT•

Have you ever hung your harp on a weeping willlow tree? In other words, have you ever lost your joy? God's people had forgotten what it was like to sing. They mourned their captivity by the rivers of Babylon. The Babylonians taunted them, saying, "Sing us one of the songs of Zion!" The people of Israel replied bitterly, "How shall we sing the Lord's song in a foreign land?" Their response reminds me of the bitter comment of a lady who was in the midst of a sticky divorce, "Don't tell me to praise the Lord—He let my husband walk out on me!"

It's hard to sing the Lord's song in a "foreign land." How many of us have been carried into situations we would never have chosen for ourselves? People who do not share our faith in Jesus Christ are always eager to see how we do in such circumstances. They expect us to handle it with Christian fortitude and serenity, and some will even be so bold as to tell us that. Somehow I think they have the right to ask us for a song. After all, if the people of God cannot make music in their misery, who can? But we will not find that song on our own. The Music Maker will have to compose it for us.

The Prophet Isaiah knew this. He exhorted the people to "hope in the Lord [to] renew their strength" (Isa. 40:31). Then he promised them they would "mount up with wings like eagles. They would run and not be weary, they would walk and not faint" (Isa. 40:31).

We have no idea how much walking, running, and flying the captives were required to do, but Isaiah took great pains in reminding them that God had not stayed home in Zion and that He would be their "stronghold in times of trouble" (Ps. 9:9). If God is the source of our joy, then the more we relate to Him, the more we will be able to relate His joy to our situations. It's easy to hang up our harps on weeping willow trees. It takes faith to take our harps down and look to God for a message in music for our oppressors.

The church today is filled with hapless harpists, or hopeless harpists, or harpless harpists—people who have hung up their joy for one reason or another. The Israelites had hung up their harps on a grief tree. The Babylonians were very cruel enemies. Describing the carnage in Jerusalem, Isaiah said, "the dead bodies are like refuse in the streets" (Isa. 5:25). It's hard to sing a song when you are grieving, isn't it? When you have watched a loved one suffer and die at the hand of cruel men, vengeance, not victory, fills the heart. Listen to the tone of the captives' complaint: "O daughter of Babylon, doomed to destruction, happy is he who repays you for what you have done to us—he who seizes your infants and dashes them against the rocks" (Ps. 137:8-9). It's at times like this that we must "wait on the Lord" who is waiting for us to wait. It may take a little time, but after a while the notes will come and He will give us something to sing about. It may not be a song in major—but then, who ever said a song in minor isn't beautiful?

The Israelites had hung up their harps on a guilt tree too. Isaiah described Israel as "a people loaded with guilt" (Isa. 1:4). The problem is, guilt doesn't know any songs and it can really make you feel miserable. People feel guilty for a variety of reasons. Some experience false guilt. I tend to be a pretty guilt-ridden person myself. I blame myself for a rainy day, a sibling's bad attitude toward another sibling, the war in Lebanon, and even the latest famine! But God is the One who will tell us if we are suffering false guilt or true guilt. People experience true guilt because they are guilty—guilty of breaking God's Laws. The Israelites honored God with their lips, but their hearts were far from Him because they had abandoned His Laws and oppressed the poor. God's forgiveness deals with our guilt. Now *that's* something to sing about!

If we wait on the Lord and confess our sins, He forgives us. Then we must forgive ourselves. Guilt is holding a grudge against yourself. Guilt wakes you up in the middle of the night and asks, "How could you do such a thing?" Or it accuses you of not trying everything within your power to make things right. "Will it ever end?" you cry. The repercussions of our sins may not end, but the guilt of them can. If there is something we are truly guilty of, and if we have fully repented, then God promises to cleanse us from it all (1 John 1:9). We need to remind ourselves that what God has forgiven us, we have no right to remember.

The Israelites had also hung up their harps on the gripe tree. "Why do you complain, O Israel?" Isaiah asked them (Isa. 40:27).

"My way is hidden from the Lord," they replied petulantly (Isa. 40:27).

When we are busy having a pity party, there is little music that can emanate from our lives. When we complain, we find our spirits overwhelmed. God offers us "the garment of praise for the spirit of heaviness" (Isa. 61:3). But we need to be within reach, if we are going to dress ourselves in that garment. I have hung my harp on this particular tree many times. The problem is, one never seems to run out of things to complain about. That is why I'm not surprised to meet many other people who have deposited their joy in the same place.

Not long ago I was visiting a ceramics class, and found myself tuned into the conversation of the girls as they worked together on their craft.

"Why don't I have a boyfriend?" compained a single girl in her thirties.

"Why don't I have a husband?" inquired a divorced friend.

"Why *do* I have a husband? I'm never appreciated! My family takes me for granted," chipped in another.

"Being a pastor's wife is so hard," I added, not wanting to be left out. "People have such unfair expectations."

"I've no friends and have such difficult neighbors," a harried woman contributed.

"My kids don't tell me enough," muttered a mother of teenagers.

"Mine tell me too much," replied her friend.

"I never have enough money," complained a young mom.

"I'm never invited to the interesting parties," confided her companion.

As I left the class that day, I felt ashamed of myself. I had allowed a complaining attitude to drown out the Master's music. I needed to wait on the Lord and ask Him to forgive me.

Whenever you reach up and take your harp from the weeping willow tree and begin to sing a song to the "Babylonians," they will be quite impressed—you'll see! When they hear you sing a song in your foreign land—be it the land of singleness, divorce, neglect, loneliness, financial distress, or unfair criticism—their attention will be caught, because such inner resources are denied to all but those who know the Lord and who wait on Him. It will make them curious. And who knows, maybe you will even have a chance to tell them about Christ.

The message the prophet gave these tuneless, depressed disciples was very upbeat. It was a word of encouragement and hope. At that moment, Isaiah seemed to be the only one singing in Zion. But then, it only takes one. Others soon pick up the melody and join in the celebration if someone starts the song. "He's waiting for you to wait," Isaiah told the sad saints. "Come back into fellowship with Him," he pleaded.

Perhaps the tree that is covered with the most harps of all is the growth tree. When we stop growing spiritually, we loose our smile, our shine, and our song. Shortly after delivering the message recorded in Isaiah 40, the prophet exhorted the people of God to look to Him in confident expectation for their deliverance. He told them that God would give them a new song to sing (Isa. 42:10). If only we would stop thinking retaliation and begin thinking restoration, then we would have new joy in our hears that would find its expression on our lips.

Are *you* all sung out? Have you lost your joy? Wait on the Lord. He is wise and wonderful. He is mighty to save. Are you worn out with grief? Wait on the Lord. God is never worn out. He is never fatigued. What's more, "He gives power to the weak, and to those who have no might He increases strength" (Isa. 40:29). Are you struggling to figure out a difficult relationship? Wait on the Lord.

A young mother once told me about the tangled web of relationships her children were caught in. She and her husband had divorced. Since then both had remarried—one of them twice. This meant that the children had a potential of eight to ten grandparents. The problem was, with that many grandparents, what were the children supposed to call them all? "You sort of run out of names," the young mom explained in exasperation, "Gram, Gramp, Nanna, Nan—where do you go from there?" What's more, how does one handle the maze of expectations built into a situation like that? The problem came into sharper focus as she told me about one family incident:

One set of grandparents was coming to visit. The young mother kept priming her three year old, "It's not Sally—it's Gram." Imagine the young mother's embarrassment when to her chagrin the child kept calling the visiting relative Not Sally!

The Israelites must have struggled with new and unexpected relationships as well. Their family structures had been decimated by war. They needed to look to the Lord. "He will give you answers to your dilemmas," Isaiah promised them. He is wise—"there is no searching of His understanding" (Isa. 40:28). God will share His secret counsel with you. After all, He is our Wonderful Counselor.

Where have you lost your joy? How will you find it again? Be strong. Do not fear. God will come and overtake you with joy. "They shall obtain joy and gladness, and sorrow and sighing shall flee away" (Isa. 35:10). So, wait on the Lord. He is waiting for you to wait.

•TALKING IT OVER•

1. IDENTIFY AND SHARE.

10 minutes

Review Psalm 137 as a group. Then individually share your response to these questions: Have you ever hung your harp in a weeping willow tree? If so, which one? Identify the arena of life that caused you to lose your joy, and briefly share it with the rest of the group.

Grief Tree   Gripe Tree   Growth Tree
   Geriatric Tree   Guy Tree   Girl Tree
   Other?

2. READ AND DISCUSS.

15 minutes

In many of the modern-day Bible translations, Isaiah 40 is written out in poetic stanzas.
- ☐ Have group members take turns reading the different stanzas of Isaiah 40. Then have each reader tell how her stanza would have been an encouragement and help to God's people who were being held captive by the Babylonians.
- ☐ Ask several volunteers to answer this question: Which verses or thoughts will be a help to *you* when you lose your joy? Why?

3. PRAYER.

5 minutes

Close in prayer, thanking God for being your source of joy and your song.

•PRAYING IT THROUGH•

Suggested Times

1. Quietly *wait* on the Lord. Concentrate on one kindness God has shown you. Thank Him for it. — *3 minutes*

2. Pray generally for joyless Christians. Then think of Christians you know personally who are joyless and pray for them specifically. — *6 minutes*

3. Read Philippians 4:4-7. Pray these verses for the appropriate people. — *7 minutes*

4. Silently pray through Isaiah 40:28-31 for yourself. — *4 minutes*

•DIGGING DEEPER•

1. Read Psalm 137.

2. What do you learn about the historical setting of this psalm from verse 1? (See also 2 Kings 25:21; 2 Chronicles 36:15-21; Jeremiah 52:26-28).

3. Why was the grief of the captives so intense?

NOTE: The grief described is not the ordinary longing for the homeland, a longing which displaced persons may always have felt. It was rather occasioned by the fact that they remembered Zion and all that that ancient capital stood for: the temple, its services, the remembrance of godly men that dwelt there, the mighty deliverances that God had wrought, the dynasty of David that had had its seat there, and the Holy City as the object of sacred pilgrimages during high festivals. All these facts would flood through the minds of captives and move them to bitter tears. (From *Exposition of the Psalms* by H.C. Leupold, Baker, 1969.)

4. What specific kinds of songs were the captives asked to sing? Why would this be such a difficult thing to do?

5. Read Psalm 42. How can Psalm 42 help us understand the way the captives felt in Psalm 137:3?

6. Read Matthew 27:41-44. How was the soldiers' tormenting of Jesus similar to the Babylonians' tormenting of the Jewish captives?

7. According to Deuteronomy 12:10-15 and 16:16, where was Israel to worship God? How might this explain the psalmist's question in Psalm 137:4?

8. Were the captives legitimate in feeling abandoned by God? According to 2 Chronicles 36:15-21, why did such a fate befall them?

9. Have you ever felt abandoned by God? When?

10. Why is disobedience dangerous?

11. What are the areas of disobedience in your life that you need to repent of?

•TOOL CHEST•
(A Suggested Optional Resource)

BIBLE COMMENTARIES
Bible commentaries are a supplement to, not a replacement for, a thorough study of Scripture. After you have read through a passage, studied it thoroughly, and drawn your own conclusions, then it is time to consult a commentary to clarify unclear passages or to get supplementary information.

There are commentaries available that cover the entire Bible. Other commentaries devote an entire volume to one individual book of the Bible. Many commentaries (especially commentaries on a single book of the Bible) give a verse-by-verse explanation of the passage, as well as information on the meaning of words in the original language (Hebrew for the Old Testament, Greek for the New Testament).

An important thing to remember when using commentaries is that they may be biased according to the author's point of view. Some commentators are better than others at presenting all the possible views on a given issue. Remember that the commentaries are not the authority—the Bible is.

Two good single commentaries on the whole Bible are: *Matthew Henry's Commentary on the Whole Bible* (Zondervan), and *Wycliffe Bible Commentary* (Moody Press).

There are a number of sets of commentaries containing single volumes on individual books by different authors. Generally, the following sets are good: *Expositor's Bible Commentary* (Zondervan). This is a fairly new set. At this point, only the New Testament is completed. The Old Testament volumes are still being written; *Tyndale Commentaries on the Old Testament* (InterVarsity Press); *Tyndale Commentaries on the New Testament* (Eerdmans); *Everyman's Bible Commentary* (Moody Press).

From an economic standpoint, it might be best to purchase a single volume commentary on the whole Bible. If you desire to consult single volumes on individual books, it might be best to borrow them from a library or from an individual who has an extensive library, as these volumes tend to be expensive ($15-$25 each). It is always a good idea to borrow and use a commentary before you buy it. But remember, do all of your basic Scripture study *before* consulting a commentary.